Traveling My Detour!

Living with Struggle and Surprise

~

Traveling By Detour!

Living with Struggle and Surprise

~

Stephen M. Gower, CSP

Foreword By: Suzanna G. Davis, M.D.

Lectern Publishing
P.O. Box 1065, Toccoa, GA 30577

First edition, published 2007 by LECTERN PUBLISHING, P.O. Box 1065, Toccoa, GA 30577. First Printing, 2007.

Library of Congress Catalog Card No.: 2007905479
ISBN: 978-1-880150-42-9

Contents

Mile Markers

Dedication

I have dedicated this book to...

Ron Seib.

A remarkable anchor of support for more than a decade,

a neighbor who blesses me with perpetual surprise,

a man wise beyond his years,

an extraordinary friend!

Foreword

I am grateful to Stephen Gower for the privilege of penning this foreword to his book, *Traveling By Detour!* As a relative latecomer to his journey, I read his book expecting to be informed and entertained. I was pleasantly surprised to view the depth of his insight in describing his long term and ongoing struggle with illness and a very human tendency towards denial.

Stephen has shown courageous openness in his speaking and publications. This helps destigmatize and demystify mental illness, and can be powerfully encouraging to others. Recent neuroimaging studies suggest a tendency in Bipolar Disorder to overfocus on minor stimuli and to struggle with processing the "big picture" of thoughts and emotions. Stephen certainly has suffered tremendously in living with illness, but has channeled that suffering into a form of ministry in reaching out to others.

I was proud to note the credit given to his wife, Lynne, for "caring enough to confront." While not always appreciated at the time, challenging resistance is vital. We would all prefer to believe that we have control where we have none, and overcoming denial is a continuous process. Mr. Gower presents a plan of actions and choices that illuminates the internal battles sufferers face.

Stephen Gower makes it clear, and I concur, that this book is not a psychiatric text and he is not an expert on psychology. This writing is a journaling of his ongoing journey away from the dangers of rationalization. Taking responsibility is difficult and courageous, requiring much discipline over thought and emotion. Insight is the first step towards change. I applaud those who walk that road, whatever their struggle in life.   Suzanna G. Davis, M.D.

Expected, Not Forthcoming

"Time ripens all things; no man is born wise."
Miguel de Cervantes

"Wisdom is the reward you get for a lifetime of listening when you'd have preferred to talk."
Doug Larson

"Growth is the only evidence of life."
John Henry Newman

~

I have resisted writing *Traveling By Detour! Living with Struggle and Surprise* for several years. The encouragement from others has been heavy. My desire has been real; but it has been thwarted by two concerns.

I have been living in a world of postponement and procrastination. My intention has been subterfuged by the two major reasons that will follow soon.

A central theme within this book is denial or illusion. For several years I have illuded myself away from crafting the words that combine to equal this book.

I have chosen to write other books, under the guise that they were more important. My deception delayed the benefit that this book would have blessed upon me. My denial delayed help for those persons who have similar struggles.

It is now time to face and address these two demons!

Traveling By Detour!

My First Expectation Equaled a Full Wellness

In the first case, I wanted to be well. The obliteration of Obsessive-Compulsive Disorder and Bipolar Disorder was to be definitive. I did not want to write about struggle, while I was still struggling.

I expected victory in the battle. Before I would write what might equal a journal of struggle and surprise, "surprise" would have had to maneuver "struggle" into a submission.

Of course, the expectation would not be met. On many occasions, my struggle with these diseases would diminish, only to later increase. The truth was: I could **expect** full healing as much as I wanted to, but in all likelihood it would not be **forthcoming**. If I waited for a full victory over the struggle, *Traveling By Detour! Living with Struggle and Surprise* would never be written.

My Second Expectation Equaled
a Full Comprehension

In the second case, I expected a full comprehension of my illnesses. Specifically, what was happening? What was unfolding - genetically, experientially, and chemically? Specifically, why were my moods swinging up and down? Why did I often experience a lateral lock, at either "up" or "down?"

Living with Struggle and Surprise

In specific terms, why was my "non-verbal stuttering" (my staying stuck) so problematic at points that included the following: one negative evaluation out of a total of two hundred evaluations, someone leaving an audience early, an office assistant popping her knuckles, and preoccupation of whether or not the coffee pot was turned off. The answers to my questions would not appear in full force. They were beginning to appear in very small increments. Again, it was an instance of expectation not forthcoming.

Let me re-state that many of the answers to these two issues (a full wellness and a thorough comprehension of the source of these illnesses) continue to be in a process of being answered. However, for the most part, that which is not forthcoming continues to overpower that for which I was wishing: a total wellness and a full understanding. I am learning to live with this.

The Mile Markers Ahead

The pages that comprise *Traveling By Detour!* equal twenty mile markers (or chapters). The next several mile markers will catalog my saga of struggle and surprise from age fourteen through age forty-two. The subsequent mile markers will share my model for traveling by detour and my observations about living with struggle and surprise. They will also re-count some of the recent detours in my journey.

Traveling By Detour!

I want to make clear that this book is personal in nature. It was extremely therapeutic for me to write and, in part, equals a journaling that my doctors have urged me to pursue for almost a decade. If this book is helpful to you and your family, then I celebrate with you.

The essence of this book is not technical or medical in nature. I have neither the inclination nor the qualifications to pursue such an activity. I want to emphasize that I am not a doctor and have no training in psychiatry and psychology. If your struggles equal anything similar to mine, I strongly urge you to seek and benefit from professional help.

It is also important to note that there are several books listed in the Books on the Subject List to which your doctor may refer you. The Books on the Subject List is located near book's end.

~

Both Diagnosed and Exhibited

"People are like stained-glass windows. They sparkle and shine when the sun is out, but when the darkness sets in their true beauty is revealed only if there is a light from within."
Elizabeth Kubler-Ross

"No one is as capable of gratitude as one who has emerged from the kingdom of night."
Elie Wiesel

"Never confuse a single defeat with a final defeat."
F. Scott Fitzgerald

~

The wall held one picture; the picture tilted to the right. The room was cold, not cold at point of temperature, but "cold" as in "there was a void of emotional warmth, no sense of welcome." When the doctor entered the room, the room appeared even colder.

Tall in structure, but not tall enough to draw attention away from his abrasive demeanor, the doctor was brutally matter-of-fact. There was no sense of compassion attached to the dispensation of his diagnosis.

I remember the diagnosis. I remember that the picture on the wall was crooked. It tilted so much that I wanted to straighten it. I shared as much with the doctor. His response bordered on ridicule, again no degree of caring, just condescension. He even admitted that he considered leaving the picture tilted, just to see how other patients would react.

Too much harshness on my part? Perhaps. But, I will never forget that picture frame. This is interesting, and important, because I have no idea what was within the frame, just that it was tilted.

This mile marker is positioned early in *Traveling By Detour!* for a reason. The crooked picture frame points to my obsession with what you might perceive as trivia. It also signals my capacity to become so driven by detour that I concentrate on "the minor." I concentrate to the degree that "the major" often becomes camouflaged or even significantly diminished by "the minor."

A Crooked Picture-Frame Ruled My Head and Heart

What mattered to me, more than the diagnosis, was the picture frame. It was not right. And as odd as it might now seem, the fact that it was wrong was actually more important to me than the fact that I was not well.

In reality, the frame that slanted in a downward direction was not as much holding the picture, as it was holding me. I was caught, trapped, stuck by four little pieces of wood. The amazing thing, now observed from a perspective of many years is this: What was happening in that room between me and that off-center picture frame, right in the midst of the diagnosis of my two illnesses, was actually more important to me than the diagnosis.

Living with Struggle and Surprise

Gradually, a horrid concoction of similar instances began to spin through my mind. These were occasions, that for the most part, I had been denying as being that abnormal: The incessant checking of the stove to be sure it was off, the repeated scrutiny of the hotel room locks, the horrific examination of any tax or insurance form, a cacophony of inspections of almost everything imaginable, and mood swings that were unexplained.

At this very point, the detours that had been dominating my life and the lives of my family raised their venom-filled fangs. Yet, for some reason I started feeling better. Right there, adjacent to the skewed picture frame, I felt better, much better. Something happened.

I have learned to call it Bipolar Disorder. Bipolar Disorder equals a mood disorder. It can sometimes take the shape of drastic and unpredictable shifts, or reversals. That was happening to me, while I was in the doctor's office, receiving and ferreting through the diagnosis.

It must be noted here that my wrestling with Bipolar Disorder has equaled a grappling with more than mere shifts of mood. Much of my hurt has also come, not from "ups and downs," but from a long period of time "in the down" (or "on the up"). The phenomenon of prolonged "downess" is addressed in the closing portion of Mile Marker Seven under the sub-heading: "The Lateral Lock."

Traveling By Detour!

Diagnosis and Manifestation Were Occurring Simultaneously

An interesting insight, blessed with a perspective of years of distance, is that two things were going on at the same time. The diseases that were being **diagnosed** in that cubicle, void of emotion, as cold as a frozen statue, were actually being **manifest** in that same room.

The stellar point is this: I identify with that fact. Not only did I recognize it from the outside; I was actually experiencing it on the inside. My mind, my mold and hold vessel, was having to process two things at once; but it had been doing that for years. Lurking behind my every breath was both a non-verbal stuttering (getting stuck) and a mood shifting (as volatile as a malfunctioning elevator, caught in a vicious up and down cycle).

Unfortunately, the malfunctioning elevator would choose to pause before abruptly starting again. My experience with the failing elevator was, that as far as I was concerned, it would pause more "in the down" mode than "in the up" mode. The lower levels of my life is where the elevator would choose to spend most of its time, locking me into a horizontal hell.

If I wanted to be specific, I was actually battling three demons: Obsessive-Compulsive Disorder, Bipolar Disorder manifest in "up and down" mood shifts, and depression that equaled a more persistent "downness" in a lateral lock.

The Expressed Equaled the Experienced

Recognition of the illnesses in the form of a diagnosis was being **expressed** by the doctor. Gradually, the reality was being **experienced** by me.

This was not occurring on two different time-poles; it was unfolding concurrently, at the same time. Upon reflection, I ponder this as remarkable.

Worded another way, what the doctor was talking about was not merely something "out there." What he was talking about was transpiring "within me."

The case the doctor and my wife were making became difficult to refute. The proof lay within the room.

The stellar development is this: At least for a brief period of time, I saw the proof. I was experiencing what they were talking about.

I was the proof. Now, the doctor's office held six elements for me: the doctor, the diagnosis, my wife, the tilted frame, me, and a choice.

I knew, at point of head and heart, that choice was at that moment the most important power in that room. I could not circumvent that fact.

Choice was caring enough to confront me face to face. Eventually, I would have to choose between two powers, Responsibility and Illusion.

~

ROI: Responsibility Over Illusion

"The price of greatness is responsibility."
Winston Churchill

"Don't put the key to your happiness is someone else's pocket."
Swami Chinmayanandaji

""I am only one; but still I am one. I cannot do everything, but still I can do something; I will not refuse to do something I can do."
Helen Keller

"Mistakes are the portals of discovery."
James Joyce

~

In financial circles, ROI means "Return On Investment." In some scenarios, there is no return on investment. In personal growth, when retreat from struggle and setback demolish pleasant surprise and satisfaction, there is little appreciation of ROI: "Responsibility Over Illusion."

One of the first dates that my wife and I took as a married couple was to the Fox Theatre in Atlanta. My wife is particularly fond of the gentleman who was performing: David Copperfield. He is an American magician and illusionist best known for his remarkable combination of illusions and storytelling.

Traveling By Detour!

Illusion Equals Deception, Even Denial

Fundamentally, illusion reveals itself as an erroneous perception of reality. Illusion is grounded in deception. There is an attitudinal shifting of a deceptive genre. The camouflaging of reality occurs in a fashion that deflects truth and crafts illusion.

When the issue is living with struggle, many of us complicate the challenge when we approach it under the illusion that the responsibility for our wellness-process lies elsewhere. There is no possibility that it lies within us. This is related to our tendency to push our blame-shifting button.

Self-Trickery Is Dangerous

Early on, in some of my bleakest hours of struggling with Obsessive-Compulsive Disorder and Bipolar Disorder, I detected within me a robust tendency to conclude that I held no responsibility for the illnesses and hence no responsibility for the healing process. I became a master at illusion or trickery, most dangerously self-trickery. Others needed to take responsibility for this situation, not me:

- If I held my family liable for my "caughtness," then my family should take the responsibility for the mess.

- If the chemicals within my brain were awry, then the chemical allocation would have to self-correct.

- If God was accountable for my illness, then God would have to take responsibility in the form of working a miracle. He created the mess in my head. He would have to clean it up - alone.

- If a mixture of my past experiences was dominating me, then those responsible for the past experiences would have to be responsible for making it better.

- If my self-esteem had been damaged to the point of serious harm, then those who took teasing to the point of torture, and rough-housing to the point of ridicule, would have to make it right.

- If the doctors just could not get their act together, if I would have to switch from psychiatrist to psychiatrist repeatedly, then sooner or later, one doctor would have to get it right.

- If my current doctor, now with me for six years, cared enough to confront my deep denial, then the one who had to do the re-thinking was her, not me.

- If the books I read led me toward a claiming of responsibility, rather than a denial of responsibility, then all the books had not been researched thoroughly. They were wrong.

Traveling By Detour!

Illusion Had Me Trapped

I was in a prison crafted by illusion. And I continued to heap chain upon chain. Illusion would continue to ensnare me in a trap of deception and denial. I was beginning to see that my choices were leading to the illusion.

Year would join year before I would choose the responsibility for my wellness-journey. Responsibility would not begin to overpower illusion until I began to choose more wisely, both from the point of attitude and behavior.

What Happened Was: SURPRISE!

As I chose to take more responsibility for my getting better, I began noticing that I was being caught by pleasant surprises. As I chose to take more responsibility for my getting better, as I chose to transcend, albeit gradually, my acts of deception and denial, I began taking tiny, progress-steps.

The Locks Became Real

I would choose to enter a psychiatric hospital in Gainesville, Georgia. The locks worked; the stench of medicine and urine was strong. The bland group therapy seemed a horrific waste of time; the visit by my pastor indicated that he felt more awkward then I did. The shock and concern that spun out from the eyes of my family was disconcerting. But again, surprise, out from it all, I was beginning to get better.

I would begin to take my medicines more regularly, then forget to take them - and blame it on the time-zone changes associated with my heavy schedule of travel. I would visit my psychiatrist/therapist every two weeks, then once a month, then every two months. She would insist that I would stick with my "every two week" schedule. I would resist.

I Felt As If I Were the Enemy

Regression would spin out from my resolution and my response. The "up and down" of it all was like a machete attacking my moods. Although reflection sends a different message, I felt as if I had no army of allies, no arsenal of resources.

Approaching me was a battalion of villains called Obsessive-Compulsive Disorder (a non-verbal stuttering, an incessant checking, a "staying stuck," and unwanted recurring thoughts). They were joined by a mammoth brigade named Bipolar Disorder (a cacophony of disharmony in my head - sounding the onslaught of unexplainable mood shifts). Everybody was aiming at me.

For the most part, I felt defenseless. I held no bow and quiver of retaliation-arrows. There was at my disposal no weaponry and no munitions store. It was not good; indeed, I felt alone beyond measure. I never really wanted to hurt myself, but if the possibility of hurt was to come my way, I am not sure that I held the energy or the desire to move.

Traveling By Detour!

Progress Was Slowly Trickling My Way

Even in the midst of the onslaught, void of any genre of weaponry, I was beginning to feel this way: "Even if there was no help on the outside, there was help on the inside. I was meandering toward a marvelous Strength within." At least in part, I had myself to thank for it...SURPRISE!

Any movement away from illusion toward the acquisition of responsibility will affirm the following:

- Illusion rests on a **slippery** and **collapsible** stage; responsibility positions itself upon a **firm** and **staid** foundation.

- Illusion **complicates** and **exaggerates** the detours associated with struggle, and even surprise; responsibility brings both **focus** and **force** to a traveling by detour.

- Illusion can **thwart** the initiative and effort to traveling by detour; responsibility can **fuel** the journey that equals a traveling by detour.

- Illusion brings **denial/deception** to traveling by detour; responsibility blesses traveling by detour with a beneficial **acceptance** and a definitive **action.**

Living with Struggle and Surprise

- Illusion can equal the **temporary**, or on occasion exhibit a longer shelf-life; responsibility routinely establishes a more solid **trend** of growth.

- Illusion equals **postponement**; responsibility leads to **pursuit.**

- Illusion, in the midst of struggle and surprise, can lead to **fatigue**; responsibility, in the midst of struggle and surprise, can lead to first **focus**, then **fulfillment**.

- Illusion **delays** and **dwarfs** a state of living (well) with struggle and surprise; responsibility **facilitates** an effort to live (well) within a crucible of struggle and surprise.

Personally, my many efforts at illuding others, and even myself, were successful. Instead of dealing with the detours thrust my way, I denied them and thus intensified their negative influence upon my life and the lives of my family. Once I chose to allow Responsibility to overpower Illusion, I began to grow. I would have to remember that authentic Responsibility would not only equal **attitude**, it also would have to embrace **behavior**.

Traveling By Detour!

Two in the Ring

There are two in the ring. Illusion (denial) and Responsibility (acceptance/accountability) fight against each other.

Responsibility must not approach Illusion ill-prepared. If Responsibility forgets that it must include both attitude and a prepared behavior, the skirmish will equal the scrawny (Responsibility) against the strong (Illusion).

Responsibility must take itself seriously (and you and I must take Responsibility seriously). We must remember that the attitude of Responsibility, minus a subsequent Responsibility-behavior, will place Responsibility in a position of jeopardy.

Illusion will manipulate Responsibility into a barrage of submission-holds. Either Responsibility will "tap out" or her corner will throw into the ring a wet and bloody towel.

However, if Responsibility walks toward the ring, buoyed by an attitude of confidence and a behavior of preparation, things will be different. If Responsibility is toned by an acceptance of an accountability for the situation, the outcome will not be the same.

Denial/Delay need not diminish Responsibility's preparation before he enters the ring. The definitive outcome lies within Responsibility's attitudes and actions.

Living with Struggle and Surprise

Denial Equals My Huge Regret

One of my mammoth regrets is that I chose to acquiesce so much control over my life to denial. One of the saddest choices I have made is to have waited until age forty-two to allow a professional the opportunity to diagnose these horrific illnesses with which I would struggle the rest of my life. (More on this subject will be covered in the next mile marker of *Traveling By Detour!*)

Perpetual postponement need not rule the roost of response-options. Procrastination can be overpowered. Denial need not wear the victor's crown.

Surprise!

The moment I began making wiser choices is when I would be caught by pleasant surprise. Once, I began stumbling toward Responsibility, and staggering toward my Army of Allies and my Arsenal of Resources, I would fare much better in the Ring of Struggle!

~

Late, But Not Too Late

"The past is but the beginning of a beginning."
H. G. Wells

"Genius is nothing but a great aptitude for patience."
George-Louis de Buffon

"The way to get started is to quit talking and begin doing."
Walt Disney

"I think a hero is an ordinary individual who finds strength to persevere and endure in spite of overwhelming obstacles."
Christopher Reeve

~

I am not among the few who chose (choose) to deny or procrastinate at the point of admitting attempts at illusion in the midst of struggle. I am among the many. I am not among the few who chose (choose) to blame any, late diagnosis upon "them" or "it." I am among the many.

For decades, others knew something was awry. They recognized that I possess the capacity to worry over the trivial, to become stuck with the insignificant, to oscillate between "a low" and "a high" within a matter of seconds.

Only upon hindsight can I recognize how my existing low self-esteem was aggravated by the following events with which I dealt poorly: 1) Being omitted from Key Club in high school, 2) being removed from the key role in the Governor's

Traveling By Detour!

Honors Program Signature Drama Production (by a Mr. America   prototype) because I did not possess anything close to the required physique, 3) hearing that my father told my mother as I walked to receive my high school diploma: "Why is he strutting so? He has not done anything," 4) being teased to the point of torture because of skinny legs and barely visible biceps.

Surprise! Even as I write these words, tears still trickle down my cheek. The truth is this: I either did not recognize these facts early on, or I denied them. Nevertheless, to this day, they still hold at least a modicum of power over me.

I recognize with a throttle of full force that low levels of (or an imbalance between) serotonin, norepinephrine, and dopamine levels could have been (and still are) part of my struggle. The question is: "Why did I choose to acquiesce to Denial so much power - until age forty-two?"

Why did I refuse to listen to others as they would bring initiative and effort to a caring enough to confront? Why did I not see the signals? And if I saw the signals, why would I become so proficient at deflecting them?

When ritual would rule and when counting and checking would reign supreme, why would I retreat from the attitude and action that required a move toward help? When emotional highs and emotional lows would swap places with each other, before I even detected that an exchange had occurred, why would I postpone any movement toward assistance?

Living with Struggle and Surprise

The psychiatrist who interviewed me, and would later share his insight with a committee responsible for monitoring my progress in graduate school, had concerns about my readiness for advancement. The committee ignored his concerns - so would I, for decades.

The professors, who monitored my Clinical Training in graduate school, expressed concern about my thinking patterns, and my response mechanisms. Why was I tardy, to the point of decades, in addressing the issue?

I Located the Culprit

Now, with the benefit of decades of hindsight, and a decade of sessions with my psychiatrists, I recognize that I am the only one who must be held accountable for my "late in life" diagnosis. I am the culprit.

There would be no reason to continue pressing the shift-the-blame button. At age forty-two, I was ready to discard the button, to throw it away. Admittedly, there would be many occasions where I would choose to attempt to retrieve my shift-the-blame button.

My determination to discard my shift-the-blame button was fickle in nature. This is attributed, in part, to the fact that these disorders are progressive in nature.

Personally, professional help in the form of visits with my doctors and a plethora of prescription medicines were beginning to help me (at age forty-two). But on many occasions, I would feel as if I was taking one step forward and two steps backwards.

Traveling By Detour!

I would get better, feel better, get worse, feel worse. But, Responsibility, both at point of attitude and behavior, was beginning to stack the overall odds in my favor.

I Would Stagger toward Growth, Then Stumble

Surprise! With detours piled upon detours, episodes of mania joining narcissistic behavior, at age forty-two I began to stagger toward a "suffering-well." My progress would never unfold in a straight-line fashion. Peaks would be short-lived; valleys seemed to have a much longer shelf-life. A staggering-forward would be met and overpowered by a stumbling.

No One Is Normal

I was learning well that "detourlessness" was an illusion - not only for me, but for everyone. I was free enough, at least temporarily far enough removed from my narcissism, that I began to notice others traveling by detour. In a broad perspective, no one is normal. No one will travel life's highway void of detour signs.

Unfortunately, I am not the only one who had denied the presence of hurt and the need for help. Others had learned well the dual-crafts of denial and procrastination.

Living with Struggle and Surprise

There Is Hope Ahead for Each of Us

Although forty-two (or thirty-two, or sixty-two), may appear as late, it is not too late. If postponement has been a point of commonality for many of us, then Responsibility both at the point of attitude and behavior, can become a trait that we honor and exhibit.

Whether it is Parkinson's or Attention Deficit Disorder, Autism or Bipolar Disorder, Tourette Syndrome or Obsessive-Compulsive Disorder, the challenge need not rule over us or over our families. We may need to live under the mantra of "late, but not too late," but hope - and help - is there. It stands poised and ready upon a three-legged stool: 1) Responsibility at the point of our attitude and behavior, 2) Assistance in the form of an army of allies, and 3) Help in the form of an arsenal of resources.

Hope may not eliminate struggle. Hope can encounter struggle and eventually can surface with an abundance of pleasant surprises.

~

Cracks Everywhere

"A ship in a harbor is safe
- but that is not what ships are made for."
John A. Shedd

"It's not what you look at that matters, it's what you see."
Henry David Thoreau

"Good people are good because they've
come to wisdom through failure."
William Saroyan

"Stubbornness does have its helpful features. You always
know what you are going to be thinking tomorrow."
Glen Beaman

~

With this mile marker of *Traveling By Detour!* I begin a more personal and specific recounting of my struggle with Obsessive-Compulsive Disorder and Bipolar Disorder. The particular years of emphasis will be age fourteen through age forty-two.

The age of fourteen is significant because it presents me with a first signal that I would be facing serious challenges. The warnings were unnoticed at first, then subtle, then more significant. I suspect that symptoms of my illness were being manifest prior to age fourteen. This is the year I can point toward a particular time slot that reflected the beginning of the challenges that would catapult into my life.

Traveling By Detour!

The age of forty-two is noteworthy. It is the year when I began viewing struggle and surprise from a   different perspective.

Age Fourteen

The monsters were playing with my head and heart, long before I knew what to call them, even before I began to recognize them as monsters. It was hell, and I did not know what hell was, nor that hell had a hold on me.

Diagnosis would come twenty-eight years later.   I would join the many who have postponed awkward diagnosis into a "late, but not too late" stage.

The Trek to Grandmother's House

The journey to Weezie's (my grandmother) always seemed shorter than the quarter of a mile that it registered. On its face, this is not peculiar. Time would speed when I headed to grandmother's home. By the time the eighth grade bell signaled dismissal, I would be anticipating Weezie's cookies. Then time would seem to fly.

I became the beneficiary of the delightful courthouse bell chiming 3:30, the inviting sound of the train departing the depot and heading for Atlanta. All seemed grand at age fourteen. But it was not.

Living with Struggle and Surprise

From the Rear View Mirror

In retrospect, however, what appeared to pass quickly at age fourteen, now looks like a long time ago. A fourteen year old should walk less than a quarter of a mile in less than ten minutes. My average walk, from the school to Weezie's, took more than twice that long.

Blessed with a look into "back then" from a "rear view mirror," I now comprehend what impacted and slowed my pace. There was a single factor that delayed my arrival at Weezie's, held back the speed of my steps.

The Impediment Was the Sidewalk

The sidewalk that led from the school to Weezie's house points to a very critical piece in my journey. It provides, not merely a path to Weezie's, but also a hint about the detours and distractions that would taint my life for decades.

To be specific, the sidewalk was problematic at the point of its cracks, tiny points of a planned parting between the slabs of concrete. I recall that I would recant to myself on a persistent basis: "Step on a crack; break your mother's back."

You must understand, albeit difficult - and I imagine perhaps even incomprehensible, that, even at age fourteen, this was not trivial. It was not a game. I actually feared that if I were to step on a crack, my mother would break her back.

Traveling By Detour!

Living under a Perpetual "Be Very Careful"

Fourteen, not forty-two, is when I should have first detected that there was something different in the way I thought about things. At age fourteen, I should have recognized that the wiring in the "mold and hold" vessel that equaled my brain, was not necessarily flawed, but was, heaping challenges upon me. Fourteen, not forty-two, is when I wish I had discovered that this challenge would eventually equal significant detours and stark distractions.

A Costly Burden

The obsession with cracks between these particular concrete slabs was not limited to these cracks. It would begin to include any crack within any concrete upon which I would walk. The burden associated with avoiding these cracks at a perpetual cost would signal: 1) a distraction-venom that was perpetual and potent, 2) an exaggerated appraisal of my control over events (often associated with narcissistic thinking), and 3) an overbearing pre-occupation with fear that would ultimately distort reality and blur potential.

At age fourteen, and probably long before, I was ill, and did not know it. I was not crazy, nor dangerous - but I was ill - and my illness would swell.

Living with Struggle and Surprise

What You Do Not Know Can Hurt You

A fourteen year old would not know (at least I did not know) that a pre-occupation with cracks between patches of concrete would prove harmful to that fourteen year old. Such a young man or woman might not recognize, in the early stage of the teenage years, that a persistent "watch out" or "do not make that mistake" would override and steal time and energy.

I certainly did not know that then. I did not know then (at age fourteen) that potential can be bruised by the thoughts I would think. I did not know then that I should not believe everything that I would think. I should have known then that "my stepping on a crack" would not inflict harm on Mama.

I did not recognize then that my "checking," whether it was checking for cracks on slabs of concrete or checking for a stove "left on," would eventually equal a checking-cancer. Something dangerous was brewing within me and I had no suspicion, no clue.

The cracks were everywhere. There was no way I could not step on any of them. I had set myself up for failure and, one could state, full blown illness. My expectations ran into the "out of line" range.

I was stuck, attempting to avoid the cracks. In reality, this crack-avoidance would become a metaphor for my suffering - and for my traveling by detour.

~

All Mixed Up, Permanently Set

*"Man's mind, once stretched by a new idea,
never regains its original dimensions."*
Oliver Wendell Holmes, Jr.

*"He who does not live in some degree for others,
hardly lives for himself."*
Montaigne

*"Creative minds have been known to survive
any sort of bad training."*
Anna Freud

*"Creativity is allowing yourself to make mistakes.
Art is knowing which ones to keep."*
Scott Adams

~

What I had was a bad case of the "what-ifs?" What if I did step on the crack? What if I did not check the stove enough? What if I did not move the tree again I had just planted and already moved twice? I was stuck and I could not maneuver myself out of the quick-sand of "what-if-ing."

I have just counted the "I's" in the above paragraph. There are five lines and six "I's." I wrote paragraph one, not knowing what would fall in paragraph two. I did not write paragraph one in such a fashion as to serve as an illustration for a point I was trying to make. The truth in paragraph one is "I"-centered, and it was not planned to be that way.

Traveling By Detour!

Age Eighteen

Four more years of "what-if" training had cursed me with an abrupt, "better than thou" demeanor. My rear view mirror now points out high levels of self-absorption and no level of concern as to how others were being impacted.

Although I was unable or unwilling to confront my "close-mindedness" at the point of the perils of "what-if-ing," I now know that, at age eighteen, it was inflicting more harm than I described in the previous mile marker: 1) A distraction-venom that was perpetual and potent, 2) an exaggerated appraisal of my control over events (often associated with narcissistic thinking), and 3) an overbearing pre-occupation with fear that would ultimately distort reality and blur potential.

The Infliction of Harm on Others

My unwillingness to confront my "what-if-ing" and other obsessive compulsive behavior transcended what is listed in the above paragraph. Again, the problem with my sentiment at age eighteen was that when I did begin to recognize the damage of my attitude and behavior, I recognized it only from a "me" perspective.

My illness was beginning to impact others in a serious fashion. It hurt my parents and my sister. I exceeded any normal threshold at the point of irritability. My tongue was quick; my spirit was tolerable at best and condescending at the worse. Apologies were few in coming. If they did come, they would be significantly diluted by my re-visiting a self-centered and irritable behavior.

Something Did Finally Get My Attention

It was the custom at the Toccoa High School to make available to each graduating senior a copy of the school's Anchor, my school's annual. It was also tradition for there to be a picture of each graduating senior with an appropriate signature line describing that person immediately underneath his or her name.

I have never forgotten, now more than forty years later, the words that were underneath my name: "Some minds are like cement, all mixed up, and permanently set."

That hurt. But it was true. And, upon reflection, the fact that "cement" at age eighteen relates to "concrete" is beyond remarkable.

I Had an Opportunity to Make
Perception My Business

At age eighteen, I was given the opportunity to recognize that all of my "what-if-ing," my resulting stubbornness and irritability, had an influence range that transcended me.

Traveling By Detour!

It is important to note that narcissistic tendencies can travel with Bipolar Disorder. It is helpful to understand those people who exhibit "narcissistic traits" as those persons to whom T.S. Elliot referred to as being "absorbed in the endless struggle, to think well of themselves." A grandiose sense of self-importance is often associated with both narcissism and Bipolar Disorder. Such has been the case with me.

In many cases, I was being perceived by my classmates at age eighteen as thinking of myself as important enough to never be wrong. Their perception was correct.

The Consequences of a Manifest Superiority

My suspicion is, upon decades of reflection, that there is a remarkable "connectedness"to be explored. My efforts to **control** my steps in relationship to the cracks in the concrete was connected to something else. It related to the perception by others that I was **controlling** to the degree that my confusion (mixed up) and stubbornness (permanently set) was what they saw when they saw me coming.

The consequences of a manifest superiority equal an exclusion, ridicule, apathy. I experienced exclusion from an abundance of clubs and projects because of perceived arrogance. I was insecure on the inside. An overkill of confidence was being exuded.

I was turning off friend after friend. I was on the bad end of ridicule, both at the point of size and skill. In other

Living with Struggle and Surprise

instances, I was worried about what others thought about me, only to discover that they were not thinking about me.

Not Then, But Now

It is important to note that I may have experienced brief glimpses of identifying with what my friends felt. However, for the most part, I was "living in a fog."

I still had little clue as to what was happening within me. I still possessed little inkling as to what was coming out from me.

I now suspect that I was so involved with me, that I could neither see within me, nor out from me. I recall now what one of the staff at Emory University had to say about student Gower: "The words he writes seem crafted more to cover up who he is than to express who he is."

At age eighteen, that was true. I was so busy at control and camouflage that it is a marvel that I survived both college and graduate school. That was then; now it is better.

~

Illusion As the Artistry of Escape

"You can't build a reputation on what your going to do."
Henry Ford

*"Either you deal with what is the reality, or you can be sure that
the reality is going to deal with you."*
Alex Haley

"The impossible is often the untried."
Jim Goodwin

*"It is not enough to be busy....The question is:
what are we busy about?"*
Henry David Thoreau

~

A review of the early part of Mile Marker Three will include a return to Mr. David Copperfield, an illusionist at the top of his craft. The artistry of illusion often includes mysterious maneuvers of escape - where a person appears bound, cut into pieces, or in another place - only to re-appear.

The business of "escape" is not limited to professionals who understand and practice illusion. I, and many others, are also familiar with the activity of escape.

It should be clear by now that the previous mile markers in *Traveling By Detour!* have stressed, in significant proportions, my struggle with Obsessive-Compulsive Disorder. There have been brief references to my Bipolar

Disorder and to the related mood swings. However, in significant fashion, I have left unexplored until now, a discussion of basic depression and its power over my life.

I have escaped such an encounter. I do not believe that this outcome has been intentional in nature. But it certainly reflects the way I have attempted to struggle with depression from an escape-perspective for most of my life. My maneuvers at escape have served to complicate my struggle and to intensify the venom that depression has thrust toward me.

Age Thirty

It was almost three decades ago when I began to recognize the "down-ness" that has colored my life. If Bipolar Disorder approaches "ups and downs" of mood swings (or a lateral-mood-lock), then my moods spent more time in the "down" position than in the "up" mode.

If an illusionist chose to cover, with a dark piece of cloth, a box that held a live person, then I could identify with that activity. I felt, and as recently as last night experienced, that depression equaled my being covered with some parcel of fabric, dark and heavy in nature. The result was a reduction in energy, activity, and a desire for relationships.

The interesting fact is this: I sought to escape that energy, activity and relationship-reduction with a "busyness" level that, on the surface, would appear paradoxical in nature. The "busyness" would not work.

Living with Struggle and Surprise

I Fought Back

If I was covered over with darkness and bleakness, I would first retreat to withdrawal. After several months, I would change my battle plan. Instead of withdrawal, I would escape with a frenzy of activity. I would cover that dark and bleak fabric with "my own cover" - escape grounded in "busyness." I would play depression's game. And, I would win the victor's crown - temporarily.

At age thirty and beyond, my resume of escape "busyness" seems overwhelming, with the benefit of hindsight. I would break record after record as a sales person. I would become: President of the Kiwanis Club, President of the Cancer Society, Distinguished Lieutenant Governor of Kiwanis, Chairman of the Northeast Georgia Heart Foundation, and Chairman of the Northeast Georgia Cancer Foundation. I would also serve as: adjunct Professor of Truett McConnell College, Lay-leader of the First United Methodist Church, Missions Chairman at the same church, announcer of athletic events, Master of Ceremony for beauty pageants, Board Member of the Northeast Georgia Campfire Council, Board Member of the local Salvation Army, and speak hither and yon.

Ultimately, I would be named Outstanding Young Man of Toccoa and Stephens County. Later, Toccoa and Stephens County would have a Stephen M. Gower Day.

Traveling By Detour!

I Was Not Fooling Myself

I knew deep in my head and heart, although not at first, that I was trying to escape something. At first, I thought, and sometimes still continue to think, that I was attempting to escape God's Call. Later I would begin to suspect that I was making an effort to escape my depression.

Others may have deemed my activity as noteworthy. It is also important to note that I was not merely busy. At almost every venture, I soared beyond success.

I do not mean to deny the absence of any purity of motive on my part. Many of my efforts were genuine. In many cases, my passion, my very heart, was at the center of a project. But in other instances, my efforts at "busyness" were a cover-up, an expression of narcissistic behavior, and a bold attempt to escape depression.

At first it seemed to work. After awhile, I would begin to detect the frailty of my efforts - because "I could never become busy enough to escape."

An escalation of activity would bring mostly temporary satisfaction. For the most part, the increase and intensity of my "busyness" would not equal any hint of a long term sense of satisfaction or fulfillment.

An insatiable appetite and search for satisfaction became my mantra. It was an unattainable goal.

When More Equals Never Enough

I was beginning to recognize that my efforts to control events and others was becoming a dominant theme in my life. I would seek to heap activity upon activity, relationship upon relationship, as a method to escape my darkness.

Somehow, I thought if I just could become busy enough, the depression would dwindle. There were some short-term dips in the depression cycle. But, as the "busyness" escalated, I began to notice that "more equaled never enough."

A Lateral Lock

To fully express my experiences with Bipolar Disorder, I have learned to think in terms that transcend "up and down" mood swings. The truth is this: On many days, and even weeks, I live more "in the down" than "on the up" (and on some days much more "on the up").

My history with depression is not merely vertical (up and down), it is horizontal (lateral). My depression is not simply a switching from good mood to bad mood; it often equals days in which the down is steady, persistent, and strong.

It is as if I feel locked "in the down," trapped under the dark and heavy curtain. To imply that my experience is simply a changing of moods would be inappropriate, indeed the establishment of illusion that would not hold.

Therefore, when I was trying to escape something, I was not merely attempting to illude mood swings. My depression did not merely equal the "up and down," it equaled an across the line, a sideways phenomenon, not a flimsy lock but a lock of steel. I was trying to break the lateral lock, the mood across broad sweeps of my life that was bleak, frustrating, and very painful. For the most part, the lateral lock would be stronger than I was. And, for the most part, I lived in "down," not "up."

It is appropriate to re-state that, on occasion, my lateral lock would clutch me at the "up" mode. This would look like out-of-control spending, an unexplained and often undetected hyperactivity, and excitement that never seemed to reach its peak.

Two Traps, Not One

I had experienced a significant revelation: I was trying to escape Bipolar Disorder, through "busyness." My "busyness" was designed to help me escape two traps, not one. Through frenzied activity, I was attempting to illude both "up and down" mood swings and the lateral lock (the hold depression had on me for an extended period of time). In this battle, I was not faring well.

One more huge revelation would be forthcoming!

~

On Stage, Off Stage

"A little learning is a dangerous thing.
Drink deep, or taste not the Pierian spring."
Alexander Pope

"Wisdom is knowing what to do next; virtue is doing it."
David Starr Jordan

"Wisdom is ofttimes nearer when we stoop
than when we soar."
William Wordsworth

"If you don't give a bit of yourself to
someone else, you are a failure."
Robert Mastruzzi

~

The work phase of my life is grounded in two activities: professional speaking and authoring books and DVD/CD material. Both of these efforts touch each other at a point of commonality. They shine the light on Stephen Gower. However, for purposes of this mile marker, the "on stage, off stage" metaphor has a dual application.

I prefer not to use stages. My choice is based upon two realities. In the first case, I do not use stages because they distance me from the audience and limit my interaction with the audience. I strongly favor the ability to move throughout the room, believing that enhances my effectiveness.

Traveling By Detour!

In the second case, I do not appreciate stages because you can fall off of them. I have engaged in such an activity on two occasions. Unfortunately, in one instance I was recorded. The client was kind enough to send me six copies of that video for purposes of sharing my craft with prospective clients.

Nevertheless, the "on stage, off stage" metaphor will be helpful from two perspectives. These two angles equal what I will refer to as "the professional life," and "the personal life."

On Stage As a Professional

There is no doubt within my mind that there is a linkage between my profession and my illnesses. I am definitely more creative, enthusiastic, effective, and even on occasion compassionate, because of my traveling by detour with my Obsessive-Compulsive Disorder and Bipolar Disorder.

As recently as last month, my psychiatrist/therapist re-stated the dilemma facing my doctors. Their desire is to treat my illnesses with appropriate medicine, medicine that is effective at the desired outcome, but not problematic to the point that it dilutes my personality and dwarfs my perspective.

Although, I am not physically on stage for most of my presentations, there is no doubt that a professional speaker is "on stage" when he or she is presenting. There is also no question that my work as a professional speaker is therapeutic for me. Most of the time, I strongly suspect that this is what I should be doing for the work-phase of my life.

I want to insert at this point, that since diagnosis I have

sensed something significant. One reason for my calling as a professional speaker (I still question this calling) is the fact that I can serve as a model for those persons who wrestle with the same detour.

If living with struggle and surprise is a challenge for another, my willingness to share my wrestling with Obsessive-Compulsive Disorder and Bipolar Disorder has proven both helpful and redemptive. Hundreds of personal conversations and e-mails have verified this fact.

Those co-sufferers, the family members and friends of those of us wounded by disease, have also benefited from my willingness to share my struggles and surprises. I should point out (and this may prove significant for many) that I am not at all embarrassed to share my struggles. No commendation is due here. Sharing, is for me a privilege, not a burden.

The Stage Lights

There is no question that the work-phase of my life is therapeutic for me and beneficial for others. There is also no doubt that my speaking in public positions me underneath the "stage lights," even when I am not on stage. Having authored eighteen books, also turns the light toward me.

This is an important emphasis. It can support the position that traveling along with the diseases with which I battle is a desire for the "lights" to be pointed toward me.

This is certainly not to suggest that other professional speakers have this identical desire to a similar degree. Many of my counterparts appear others-centered in an authentic fashion. However, each would also agree that, in our profession it is essential that confidence finds us.

My desire to function under the "stage lights" has not been, in every circumstance, a healthy desire. I appreciate my clients and there is no query in my heart that I serve them well. I do not lack confidence at the point of character or competency. I do, however, confess that there is a narcissistic tinge to living "underneath the stage lights."

I wrestle daily examining my desire for being in a position underscored by "stage lights." On most days, I live with a peace that blesses both me and my audience.

On Stage As a Person

What is much more problematic than my being on stage as a "professional" is my desire to be on stage as a "person." This is part of the illness with which I have lived. As a person, I persistently wrestle with: "Where is the line between expressing one's full personality and 'being special?'"

Until now, I have resisted the tendency to bring my parents into this book-equation. I have referred to them in passing, but have not emphasized their influence on my life.

It is appropriate for me to begin by stating that my parents had a positive and negative influence on me. Therapy and struggle within, has brought me to this conclusion.

I do not love my parents any less because of this. I will also be quick to admit that I have had both a positive and negative influence on my children.

I am now ready to catalog the positive and negative elements of my parents' effect on my life, as I now understand it. I want to emphasize that I understand with a full-force throttle that my parents did the best they could. I speak with pride, not with shame, their names.

The First of Two

I am the first born of my parents' two children. My father passed away when I was eighteen years of age. My mother passed away when I was fifty-three.

My mother was a college graduate. My father finished two years of college. Both were of the Christian faith. My grandmother, perhaps the most influential person in my life from a positive perspective, was my mother's mother.

I take joy in sharing the many positive influences my parents had upon my life. Recounting them is not a complex task. I look forward to writing these next paragraphs.

Mama and Daddy provided for me well. Daddy always wanted money in my pocket. Mama made sure I wore nice, clean, and well-pressed clothes.

I can go back no further than age five in cataloging what I remember about my parents. I do remember that the early years appeared grand.

I would play in bed with Mama and Daddy, we would dine and eat around a wooden kitchen table. (My hand is on that very table as I write these pages.) I felt comfortable growing up at 155 Hayes Street in Toccoa.

I recall how excited I was to secure my bicycle and rush up to the corner of Hayes and Big A Road. I would meet Daddy when he came home for lunch, and after work. Even on a cold, winter afternoon, I would be warmed by his marvelous smile.

I continue to remember Daddy's desire to insert into me athletic skills. He would hire Al Westmoreland, "Mr. Athleticism in Stephens County" to attempt to help me learn how to throw and catch a ball. Al was unsuccessful.

I remember the countless scouting events and fishing trips with Daddy. I recall the conversation where he attempted to educate me about intimacy between man and woman.

My memory now touches an eternal moment where he kissed me and wished me well in an Atlanta elevator prior to my FCC Licensing Test. He then started crying.

It pains me to say this, but I do not recall much about Mama until age fourteen. I do recollect that Mama taught public speaking from our home; and she excelled in that arena of her life. She was beautiful in person, warm and kind. I remember no tangible, negative influence from Mama prior to age fourteen.

Back to Age Fourteen

At age fourteen, some havoc would begin to unfold. Daddy would become a traveling salesman, away from home every night. Mama's own challenge with mental illness would appear dimly, but more clearly years later.

Perhaps the most difficult moments in those early years, beginning with age fourteen, equaled a "tornness" that I would feel on Friday afternoons. Right when I was eager to meet Daddy upon his return, Mama would be ready to re-count all the mistakes I made in the earlier part of the week. There would be particular tension on my part about her sharing with Daddy any conflicts I had with my younger sister.

Simultaneously, almost any given Friday night, I wrestled with the tension between anticipation (Daddy's return) and anxiety (Mama's re-counting). I feel guilty as I write this, and I suspect I felt guilty every time Daddy would return.

I now feel that Mama was doing the very best she could. As I will indicate later, she was dealing with her own depression. I certainly can identify with her at this point. I will address it further in this next section.

Two Significant Complications

It is important to note, and I will never forget, that Daddy was struggling with, and would soon die from, a heart condition. So, fully aware of his ailing heart, I would either attempt to exhibit restraint when speaking my piece, or feel guilty when I did speak my piece.

It is also important to state that Mama was wrestling with her own health problems. She would have to endure several serious treatments, particularly with what I suspect was her own depression. Whereas her depression would seem to get better over the years, mine would swell. Whereas she began to exhibit much more warmth and concern, I would choose to exhibit less.

Put Him On a Special Stage

In the midst of all of this, and especially upon later reflection, it became obvious to me that my parents' intentions were not evil, or totally self-serving. With love, and I'm sure for their own reasons, my parents wanted me to be special. In my teenage years, I never succeeded.

The Eagle Scout Award would never happen, dating the right girl would never occur. Looking like Bill or Craig would never equal a reality.

I now know they were wishing the best for me for the right reasons, and for the wrong reasons. And I honestly feel, the right reasons overpowered the wrong reasons.

But the truth is this: I could not live up to their expectations. The light that they wanted to shine on me would remain dim, or even in the "off" position. When I was on exhibit, when I was the showcase, when I was on a lighted stage, the best "me" would never show up.

A Strength Taken Too Far

Mama and Daddy desired that I be who I was; that is good. Mama and Daddy would not stop there however. I believe Mama and Daddy wanted me to be special, very special. That was not for my good. I do not mean to hold them accountable for my choices.

I will share the observation that a young teenager may choose to acquiesce an inordinate amount of his choosing-powers to his parents. I feel better saying that is what I did.

Perhaps it is as simple as their wanting the best for me and for them - and wanting it to the point of hurt. "A strength taken too far" may well describe what was occurring.

Mama and Daddy wanted me to be special. I chose to try to be special. I failed, miserably so. Placed upon lighted stage after lighted stage, I earned bad reviews; but the battle was not over, I would eventually get it right - or at least I would try as hard as humanly possible.

But Oh, If They Could See Me Now

Now, thousands of presentations and eighteen books later, they might feel better. I might feel better. But I do not feel better simply because of any accomplishments I have made.

First off, whatever I have done, has occurred with His help and with help from a battalion of family and friends. I have been the particular beneficiary of a loving and courageous wife - one who, fortunately cares enough to confront.

If my parents wanted me to be who I could be, then finally that is beginning to happen. There has been occurring for several years, albeit with a shifting back and forth within my head and heart, what I will refer to as a significant re-thinking.

Being, Not Doing

My journey, for several years and even through the writing of this book, has included a remarkable examination. I have been pondering how I think about myself at the point of attitude and behavior. I have been asking myself the two specific questions: "Am I allowing depression the power to answer the issue?" Or, "Am I resolving the issue?"

The issue of Advantage: Gower versus Advantage: Depression will surface later in the book. At this point, it is sufficient to note that I am thinking (and even acting) with a greater emphasis on Being than Doing.

This has been, and continues to be, a mammoth battle for me. I have been well-trained to think doing: by my parents, by my cycle of education both at the undergraduate and graduate levels, by my brief encounter with the military, and even by my sales-oriented work.

Mama Begins to Rise to the Occasion

Any discussion of "On Stage, Off Stage" must conclude with an emphasis on the transformation that occurred within my Mama when I turned eighteen. My mother was a drama teacher. The stage was important to her. But, at eighteen, my being on stage seemed to become a little less important to her.

There were many days when she fell into the "Stephen is special" trap and the "exhibit Stephen" modes. But just as I had my battles, she had her battles. She was winning many.

Indeed at age eighteen, I began to detect that Mama was different. It is not by coincidence that this is the same year that Daddy died.

From age eighteen on, until Mama's death at my age, fifty-three, I remember her as amazingly supportive, remarkably generous, deeply compassionate. (Again, I must stress that, although she would have significant lapses and reversals, Mama was starting to rise to the occasion. She was beginning to win her battle against depression - just when I should be expecting more defeats at the hands of depression.)

From age eighteen, up until age forty-two, Mama was marvelous. When the diagnosis occurred at age forty-two, and for the rest of her life, Mama was stellar. I write these words not to soften any prior statements about Mama. These words of affirmation are true. Any camouflage about this wonderful woman was coming off - both on and off the stage.

~

A Choice for Change

"Things do not change; we change."
Henry David Thoreau

"They always say time changes things,
but you actually have to change them yourself."
Andy Warhol

"Choices create circumstances; choices confirm
circumstances; choices change circumstances."
SMG

~

In one of my previous books, *Mountains of Motivation: How to Motivate Yourself and Create a Motivational Environment for Others* (Chapter 2), I make an observation that I want to re-state and re-phrase in this particular mile marker. It will prove helpful in exploring, in general, the power of choice, and in particular, the choices I made beginning at age forty-two, the year of diagnosis.

In the book, I refer to the military jargon of "Attention, About Face, Forward March" as a helpful model for motivation. I choose to apply that same phrase to the opportunity presented to me when I was diagnosed with Obsessive-Compulsive Disorder and Bipolar Disorder. It has proven helpful in setting a workable approach for me. It has helped me explain to others what happened within me, starting with the diagnosis.

Traveling By Detour!

Age Forty-Two

The diagnosis from the doctor, albeit from a doctor void of people skills, caught my attention. On my struggle-clock, age forty-two is highlighted as the attention-getting year.

Of course, the attention-getting gave me an opportunity to respond, or to ignore. This is not the only time I have met "attention, about face, forward march" opportunities.

When I calculated all the hours I was wasting on airplanes, I could choose to ignore or respond to the "attention-getting" within that unbelievable number of hours. I chose an "about face." I proceeded on a "forward march" goal to write a book a year for the rest of my life. Now eighteen years later, I have written eighteen books.

In another instance, when I had my heart attack and open heart surgery, I had a choice. I could let that catch my attention; I could proceed with an "about face" toward diet and exercise; I could make a "forward march" toward health. I chose to do just that.

At age forty-two, I could accept or deny the following: "Choices could create my circumstances; choices could confirm my circumstances; choices could change my circumstances."

I do not mean to imply that I always accepted this above reality. Acceptance would often be interrupted by postponement, procrastination, and denial.

Living with Struggle and Surprise

I recognize that some would include, embarrassment as an interruption in their growth-process. In all honesty, embarrassment never entered the equation for me. As I have mentioned earlier, I have no trouble referring to my illnesses in my own town, anywhere within our country, or overseas.

I also understand that we do not all possess the same starting points; neither do we all learn at the same pace. For some, facing their traveling by detour nightmare, then talking about it in public, is out of the question. I respect that position.

Personally, although I am aware that excessive vulnerability can equal manipulation, my openness about my illnesses has not been problematic. I have experienced a warm reception from my audiences and from my neighbors. There has been no stigma.

Openness Can Birth Initiative

The above sub-heading is interesting because it presents another truth: Initiative can birth openness. What must be understood here is that once I became open with myself, and open with others, I took the initiative to seek help.

At age forty-two, although my wife was pulling me all the way toward the doctor, I still had the power to resist. I was open enough within myself to recognize a serious challenge. My move toward the doctor was a wise choice. It set in motion a series of subsequent choices that would enable me to travel by detour and live with my struggles and surprises.

Traveling By Detour!

Surprise!

What I had feared (seeing a psychiatrist) would actually surface as a blessing (a movement toward wellness). What I finally felt as an obligation to seek help would lead to an opportunity to grow.

If seeing a psychiatrist was a wise, but difficult, choice, then it would lead to other wise, but difficult, choices. The surprise was this: "My resistance level was not steady. Neither was my acceptance level steady. But acceptance of the need to see a psychiatrist began to over power resistance. I was somewhat jolted at that point."

"Resistance" had been a characteristic of my demeanor for decades. It was certainly not always a negative trait. But, on occasion, it certainly possessed negative tones.

I would have expected that resistance would have played stronger roles in relationship to my subsequent visits to the psychiatrist. Oh, I would continue to "hem and haw" with my wife. Resistance, however, did eventually hold much less power over me.

The war with Resistance was not being waged by me alone. I have established that my Heavenly Father, family, friends, and a legion of clients have serviced my journey.

When I refer to the fact that I was not waging the war alone, I am not speaking of my Army of Allies. I appreciate every one of them, but they are not the subject of this segment.

Living with Struggle and Surprise

My quiver of response-arrows held an arrow that provided me with what I so desperately need. I am a structure-based person. If I was to travel by detour and live with struggle and surprise, then I needed a structure of response.

I knew I needed the doctors. I understood that I needed the medicine. I recognize that I required structure!

I Knew What I Needed

There were times when number one on my "wish list" was a structure for response. I knew how I functioned. At age forty-two, post diagnosis, I knew I would require a model.

When I began to soar beyond success, as a sales person and as a leader, it was because I blessed myself with structure. I knew where I could turn if I needed any reassurance that structure would work for me.

"Where I could turn" was "my speeches" and "what I had written." The first clue that leads to my appreciation for structure is found within how I would think and act when speaking and writing.

Hundreds of hours of teaching public speaking in the classroom, on a college level, and thousands of presentations had taught me something significant: Void of structure, I am not coherent, creative, powerful, and effective.

If I wanted my students to succeed at speaking in public, then I knew they had to have structure - organization, the bones that equal an outline, the meat on bones that equaled narratives, statistics, comparison, and contrast.

Traveling By Detour!

I wanted my students to appreciate the structure of a five room speech house; Introduction, What, Why, How, Conclusion. I could not teach structure if I did not have "structure to give." As a professional speaker, I would never receive positive evaluations and hundreds of referrals if there was not structure in my presentations.

Throughout my writings, I knew that structure worked. I understood the effectiveness of systemic approaches. I valued the foundation of a sentence and I loved to craft structured paragraphs.

As a salesperson, the reason I broke sales records was because of the proposal-organization that confounded the competition. In my commercials as a broadcaster, I was able to surpass goal after goal because I brought a rare structure to those commercials.

A Respect for Structure

There was a history behind my appreciation for structure: Out from the classroom, from behind the sales desk, within speeches and written articles. For the past many years, my appreciation for the power of structure has been deep.

I recognize that we do not have the same starting point and we learn at different paces. But I do coil up inside when I hear presentations void of structure.

What I had used to speak and write, to sell and to lead could now be used to help me travel by detour and live with struggle and surprise. Structure stood ready.

Structure in Action

Now, with the onset of diagnosis, I possessed an opportunity to bring structure to task. I knew by now, from a historical perspective, that I would be able to stack the advantage-odds in my favor when I brought a "structure in action" to my traveling by detour and my living with struggle and surprise. I was in need of a model, a method, an approach-strategy. It was forthcoming.

Beyond Resistance

The mile markers ahead will catalog my steps beyond resistance. They will place in full view the five-step model that has helped me move beyond initial diagnosis.

~

Structure: Model 5A

*"Planning is bringing the future into the present so
that you can do something about it now"*
Alan Lakein

*"Let our advance worrying become advance
thinking and planning"*
Winston Churchill

*"Unless commitment is made, there are only
promises and hopes; but no plans."*
Peter F. Drucker

*"Those who prepare for all the emergencies of life beforehand,
may equip themselves at the expense of joy."*
E. M. Forster

~

Something will become apparent in the latter pages of this book. Gardening is one of my deepest joys, a most honored privilege, and an extremely effective therapy.

Recently, my fourteen year old gardening helper and I implanted into North Georgia's terra firma (a ground that was really not that firm) two posts. They were positioned as an entrance into the walkway that led into the various-garden rooms. At the top of each post we attached a basket of Swedish Ivy.

Traveling By Detour!

Before finishing the project, and calling it a day, I suggested to my young colleague that we needed to secure the ground around the posts. It was my intent to build a support structure of well-packed North Georgia red clay. This clay can almost harden itself into brick.

I would take responsibility for solidifying the post to the right of the stones that comprised the walkway. My counterpart would be accountable for making sturdy the post to the left of the walkway.

We each addressed our post by filling in the hole that held it with an accumulation of North Georgia's red clay. Our approaches were very different.

My precious young friend transported his dirt from the left of the hole into his hole with broad sweeping motions with his hands. That was the extent of his effort. I did not address him at this point.

My strategy was not similar to his. I would return the dirt to its hole, and press it down before adding another layer. This "packing down" process would occur layer after layer.

When I felt my structure of support was near completion, I would pack with full vigor another time and add even more dirt. Finally, I would press down with the handle end of a shovel one more time, leveling the ground even with the surrounding landscape.

I decided that we would leave the posts as they were, one with very little support, the other solidly entrenched. We retrieved our post digger, yard stick, and support tools and chose to call it a day. The plans were that we would return to the garden the next morning and tackle other projects.

A Tale of Two Posts

During the summer of this particular activity, Northeast Georgia, like the rest of the country, was experiencing a horrid drought. The city had imposed restrictions on water-use. My garden had been deprived of rain for two solid weeks.

That night, Mother Nature acted as if she wanted to compensate for the drought with one mammoth down pouring. The rain was welcome but its force was overwhelming.

The next morning, before picking up Brent, I chose to make a trek toward the posts. Upon my approach I noticed one post standing solidly, the other post had a gaping hole at its surface, in places many inches deep. A slight touch would precipitate a significant wiggle. I left the poles as they were.

Later the two of us would head toward the garden for our work of the day. As we walked up the hill, I said to Brent, "I want you to look at this. Do you see any difference in the way these two posts stand?" He replied, "Yes sir." He then began to add more dirt into the area that surrounded his post.

At that point, I said, "Sit down a minute. Let's talk. There is a reason why the pole to the right survived the night with little impact from the storm. There is a reason why the pole to the left lost the battle with the storm."

Traveling By Detour!

I continued, "Now let me make clear: At your age, if I had installed your post, it might now be laying on the ground. I was not nearly as good with garden-work at age fourteen as you are. But, I would like to make a suggestion.

"The next occasion you install a post like this, take the time to build around it a solid structure of support. This post is similar to life. In life, heavy downpours will come. When they do come, a structure of support that you have built will help you make it through the storms."

We All Travel By Detour

I have invested several pages with this opening narrative. This mile marker of *Traveling By Detour!* is extremely important.

The "tale of two posts" not only offers lessons of discovery and re-discovery for Brent and me. It presents a universal truth for every man and woman who journeys through life. The application-significance of the concept behind this mile marker is extremely broad in scope.

The lesson Brent learned that day will, I hope, become forever etched in the mind that equals his "mold and hold vessel." It is my desire that he will file the "structure of support" concept deep within his head and heart.

Living with Struggle and Surprise

Traveling By Detour Necessitates a
Structure of Support

I have no knowledge about the detours that you have faced, are experiencing, or will encounter. I am acutely aware that your detours may not include Obsessive-Compulsive Disorder and/or Bipolar Disorder (my detours). I do know that your detours have an impact upon you, your family, and your friends.

We all travel by detour. We also travel by different detours. Levels of difficulty may not appear the same, but to the person involved, the challenge may equal significance.

There is a point to be established and celebrated. The detours we experience may be different in nature, but we have something in common with all who travel by detour.

What joins each of us together, as we seek to live with struggle and surprise, is that each of us will benefit from a structure of support. The most effective way to move from an "Advantage: Detour" scenario to an "Advantage: Me" position is to establish and implement a structure of support.

If we just haphazardly, without the benefit of plan and method, heave dirt back into the hole of our frustration, we will complicate the situation. If, however, we choose to address the post within the hole (our detour) with a structure of support, we stack the odds in our favor.

Traveling By Detour!

If we bless ourselves with layer of strategy, solidly packed upon other layers of strategy, we will gift ourselves with a spring-board for response, a launching pad for traveling by detour. We will overcome the flimsy, with the solid.

Organization will prevail over disorganization. A construction of a support mechanism, a composition of strategy and follow-through, will over power the haphazard.

Fill in the Hole That Resembles Your Detour with That Which Equals Your Structure of Support

The next five mile markers will catalog a model of structure that has enabled me to understand this next sentence with a full-force throttle. The post-in-the-hole analogy has helped open the door to a traveling by detour. It has pointed the way toward living with struggle and surprise.

It has benefited me beyond measure. It is also important to note that it has not always benefited me. There have been moments when I have forgotten this strategy of support. There have been other occasions when I thought about it, but failed to implement it.

I cannot overstate this fact. I have not been perfectly faithful to my Model 5A Structure of Support. But when I have chosen to be faithful, when I have chosen to retrieve it and implement it, my journey of traveling by detour has been well serviced.

The key word in the previous paragraph is "chosen." My structure of support is of no benefit to me unless I choose to "think of it" and choose to "implement it." My "thinking of it" has never actually benefited me, unless I have chosen to "implement it." The "thinking of" minus the "implementing" equals a farce, not a force.

The Model 5A

It will be helpful for us to identify the model 5A before we address it in the subsequent five mile markers. An advanced knowledge of the structure that is to follow, will reveal the glue that binds the mile markers to each other.

The five key words that will unite these next five mile markers are: Anticipate, Accept, Analyze, Apply, Appreciate. They will be addressed, and must be comprehended, as steps that lead to each other.

The sequential nature of this model is not to be taken lightly. Each phase is built upon the previous step.

Anticipation will set the stage for Acceptance. Acceptance is a pre-requisite for Analysis. Analysis will define and support Application. Application, if authentic and effective at the point of journey servicing, will give birth to a spirit of Appreciation, not for the detour, but for the process at work. Appreciation will equal much more than a back-end response, it will validate the process and boomerang back toward Anticipation.

~

Anticipation, Not Shock

"Life is largely a matter of expectation."
Horace

"I run on the road, long before I dance under the lights."
Muhammad Ali

"A goal without a plan is just a wish."
Antoine de Saint-Exupery

"The anticipation lessens the sting."
SMG

~

As a young child, I learned to associate anticipation with excitement. I would expect the snow that would fall tomorrow, canceling school. "Soon Daddy and I will go fishing" was an expression of anticipation.

When decades started to pile upon each other, my inner-life cupboard of comprehension started to expand. It began to hold an understanding of anticipation that had broadened, swollen enough to include dread.

I would learn to think of anticipation in different terms: the dentist's impending shot of novocaine, the onslaught of adrenaline-withdrawal after a series of presentations, the event of tomorrow's open-heart surgery.

Traveling By Detour!

Another Arrow in the Quiver

For several decades, my definition-quiver held only two descriptions for anticipation. It meant either "excitement" or "dread." That simple polarization allowed for a convenient structuring or comprehension.

Anticipation would, at that point, equal a composite of "either or" scenarios. The possibilities would equal: The foretelling of good or bad, the announcement of pleasure or pain, the advent of exhilaration or the unfolding of frustration and disappointment.

It is only within the last twenty years that I have recognized (and addressed) that anticipation has more to offer than either excitement or dread. Anticipation can also equal that which is preparatory in nature. This third arrow within the quiver of definitions is not unrelated to its companions (excitement and dread).

The full force of excitement can mean more for you if you have prepared for that big day or moment. For sure, serendipity is a stellar blessing, but preparation can amplify all that excitement has to offer. Preparation enhances the pleasure, allows you to savor the grand, to celebrate the expected.

Preparation (the third definition of anticipation) can also inform your journey when your anticipation equals dread. You know that potential for a challenge is coming, and you prepare for it. Your preparation touches you at the point of your dread. The touch is helpful. Anticipation as preparation lessens the sting of anticipation as dread.

A center piece of my traveling by detour is this: I have learned that my detours are less painful, less pervasive, when I anticipate them.

In a broad sense, my anticipation has served as an element of defense. I do not refer to defense as "escape," but celebrate defense as "preparation."

This is precisely what defense does for me. It allows me to diminish or diffuse (not deny) the surprise that my illnesses are planning to throw my way.

My illnesses are strong enough without the complication of "surprise." Their arsenal is powerful against me. But by expecting their onslaught, I diminish their potency.

The Tool of Detour-Anticipation

Specifically, the instrument of "detour-anticipation" has benefited me in numerous instances. It will be helpful if I catalog some specific detours that I have learned to anticipate because of my past experiences and my mistakes.

Detour-anticipation is an important first step in the previous mile marker - *Structure: Model 5A*. Remember, anticipation will lessen the sting of the detour.

The examples that follow may not be relevant for your particular situation. I list them to illustrate, in a plethora of instances, the force of anticipation.

Traveling By Detour!

Medicine: When All Else Fails, Read the Instructions

The mistakes I have made in regards to taking my medicine are many. My prior mistakes have led to a greater emphasis on preparation at the point of anticipation.

I have learned to anticipate what will happen when I do not "follow the instructions." I have educated myself to think like this: "If I do not take my medicine on time, or forget to take my medicine, this is what I can anticipate happening."

The issue of taking medicine on time has presented me with an opportunity for rationalization (a very dangerous activity). I have rationalized, inappropriately so, that my traveling across the country, and in and out of the country, has presented me with insurmountable challenges.

I have told myself: "These time zone challenges give me an excuse for not taking my medicines on time." I know better; I know that I can make the choice to be more disciplined. I am making much progress in this area.

But when I falter, when I delay taking my medicine, or when I refuse to take it at all, I have learned to anticipate the consequences. This anticipation of the consequences has been very helpful and therapeutic in nature.

If I do not take my medicines as I should, I have learned to anticipate an increase in my obsessive thoughts, an escalation in my up-down mood swings, and the lateral lock that equals a more persistent dark and heavy curtain of depression.

Living with Struggle and Surprise

My "not taking my medicines as I should" has produced for me, and for my family and friends, undesirable consequences. My failure to anticipate the impact of my inappropriate choices upon my family and team members has been significant.

By following the instructions on the prescription bottle, and from my doctor, I exhibit better choices. I decrease my bouts of obsession, abrasive irritability, and a thriving on confrontation that is problematic, to say the least, for my family. Not taking my medicines at prescribed times is a selfish gesture on my part.

Anticipation leads toward a healthy retreat from a havoc of unnecessary manifestations of my illness. The anticipation of what might happen, by "not taking my medicine as I should," is not only healthy, it is also helpful. Anticipation whispers in my ear words of preparation: "Plan to take your medicines as instructed. Execute your plan. Follow the instructions."

Caffeine and Chocolate: A Tag Team of Escalation

I love chocolate and will confess to appreciating caffeine. But, I have learned to prepare myself for what happens when I "cheat a little" and partake of either caffeine or chocolate. "What happens" is this: Although I do not understand the particulars, caffeine and chocolate rush my medicine through my system, diminishing its effectiveness.

Traveling By Detour!

My levels of frustration and anxiety increase. Being around me is a challenge.

By preparing to stay away from them both, and anticipating any violation-consequences, I stack the odds in my favor, not in the favor of my illnesses.

Fatigue: A Major Irritant

When I am tired, when the airplane schedules are more than I can take, I have learned to anticipate the detour that equals more than a small dose of irritability. Anticipation has birthed preparation in a manner that is simple to illustrate.

Because I allow fatigue to have too much power over me, and because my wife and I have anticipated the consequences, we have agreed on a course of action. This procedure has been in effect for many years.

Upon returning to the Atlanta or Greenville airports, and often before departing, I spend the night in an airport area hotel. This has worked, and is working. My rest has been calming for both of us. This is a classic example of what can happen when anticipation (expectation of irritability) marries preparation (a night at the airport hotel).

Good Can Be for Bad

One of the areas in which I get stuck is "religion." I recognize that my Obsessive-Compulsive Disorder (the recurrence of unexpected and unwanted thoughts) has a huge

Living with Struggle and Surprise

hold on me here: "If I do not do this act of personal sacrifice, I will go to hell."

I know better, and can share with others, that this is not Christ-centered thinking. He has taken care of "what I think I can take care of." This will be addressed in more detail in a mile marker near book's end that is entitled *Grace Who?*

There are certain television programs that fuel my illness at this point. Invariably, I will take something out of context, latch upon it, and obsess over it.

The implication is simple here. Because I can anticipate the power of these programs over me, I have decided not to watch them. This too has worked for me.

It is as if there is another whisper, quietly speaking into my ear: "Don't go there." Once again, anticipation plus preparation equals the avoidance of serious consequences.

It is helpful to note that religion is one of four major areas of "becoming stuck." The other areas are: Money, sex, and politics.

Closer Than They Appear

It would be less than authentic, and far from honest if I did not begin to address my march with, and against, mania. I will be addressing mania as an impulsive and intensive slot of time when I am basically approaching an out-of-control state.

As I understand it, there are different levels of mania. I identify most with those levels that will include different layers of a racing mind, heightened activity, impulsive and excessive spending.

Traveling By Detour!

There is one particular insight about my relationship to my mania that I must share. When it is at its worse, I am not sure that I see it coming. I even doubt the fact that I am always aware of my mania when it is in full force.

Today, most every car on our highways carries a small inscription on the side-view mirror: "Objects in mirror are closer than they appear." This is a helpful reminder.

I have learned to anticipate that mania is always lurking in the background. Although I may not know specifically when it is getting ready to attack me, and even that it is attacking me, I have learned to anticipate that mania is out there, or within me, primed for an assault.

Mania opportunities are always closer than they appear to me. My wife calls it like it is; and believe me she does this with an intense directness.

I resent and resist the fact that someone else thinks mania has a hold over me, strong arming me into a submission-hold. I fight back, only to discover on later reflection that another's diagnosis was correct.

After many years of battling mania, I have learned to target my most vulnerable moments. I have also acquired an ability, far from consistent, to build response-defenses when I detect the onslaught of vulnerable moments.

The Holidays Can Be Terrible

My battle against depression in general, and my bouts with mania in particular, intensify during the holidays. I

Living with Struggle and Surprise

recognize that I am not alone at this point. I continue to wrestle with why holidays are so problematic.

I know that the polarity of the apparent happiness of others is a stark contrast to the loneliness that I sense during holidays. My wife has proven to be very sensitive at this point and has helped me prepare for the onslaught of the holidays. She prepares special trips and activities for me to help me cope with the stress of the holidays.

We are aware that holidays present challenges and have learned to prepare for the mania-triggers that may present themselves. We know what to anticipate. Our anticipation leads to preparation. In many cases, it helps.

Sales Can Be Costly

When my mania is even at its lowest level, when impulsiveness merely starts the walk into my door, I know that I should have one attitude towards sales: "Do not go there!"

If our store for men on the downtown mall has a two-for-one sale on shirts, I will make it ten-for-five. The savings of $200 seems to justify an expenditure of $200. When two shirts would have equaled plenty, ten shirts equaled a problem. Mania threw me and my spending overboard.

When Spring arrives and my intensity for gardening is pervasive, I over-spend. I will not buy hundreds of seeds; I will buy thousands at sale prices. I will not buy a couple of azalea plants; I will purchase thirty azalea plants at sale prices. Because these things are "on sale," the purchase seems justified.

Traveling By Detour!

Our yard holds thousands of daffodils and hundreds of day-lilies - but I bought every one of them on sale. The concoction of plants in my garden looks more like a nursery.

A glance into my garden will cause me to see beauty. My wife would say: "I see obsessive compulsive behavior. You are stuck."

If there is a land developer on Hilton Head Island offering "development prices" on lots that have investment potential, I should not go there. I did "go there" once. It would have been prudent and seemingly profitable to purchase a lot, perhaps even two lots. But, not for me.

In the midst of mania, I purchased many lots, failing to factor into my investment-equation the loan-interest, property taxes, and association dues. It almost broke us financially.

Sales and investment opportunities present challenges for me. I have learned to anticipate the consequences of my poor choices. My anticipation has lead to preparation. When sales are on, I do not go there - to the sales.

This exemplifies how anticipation can be both preventative and preparatory in nature. Anticipation is a powerful weapon in my war against mania. It is part of the arsenal for an on-going battle - not a win or lose conflict.

Much of this section has been written in the present tense to reflect that I still am in the fight. I have not lost the fight, neither have I won the fight. The battle is continuous.

Living with Struggle and Surprise

Surprise

There is no doubt in my mind that I will be fighting this battle for the rest of my life. But there is a pleasant surprise in the mix. I am winning much more than I am losing. As long as anticipation stands in my corner, I feel as if I have an edge.

Anticipation equals a partner in my struggle. Anticipation is my ally, not my enemy.

The Shock Factor

The detours you travel will sting you less when you anticipate what lies ahead. Be careful here. Anticipation taken too far can equal an incessant "what-if-ing."

The critical fulcrum of this mile marker is an invitation to consider opportunities that will help you minimize the shock factor that is often associated with traveling by detour. A key word in the prior sentence is "minimize."

"Minimization," not "elimination" is a key component of *Traveling By Detour!* Anticipation will not eliminate struggle within your life. Anticipation may not significantly alter the degree of your struggle. It can, however, be helpful - even if it leads only to a "minimization."

The anticipation lessens the sting.

~

Acceptance, Not Denial

"We cannot change anything until we accept it.
Condemnation does not liberate, it oppresses."
C. G. Jung

"Conditions for creativity are to be puzzled;
to concentrate; to accept conflict and tension;
to be born everyday; to feel a sense of self."
Eric Fromm

""I will love the light for it shows me the way, yet I will
endure the darkness because it shows me the stars."
Og Mandino

"Acceptance does not equal a bland acquiescence.
Acceptance equals the first step of assertiveness."
SMG

~

I had just finished keynoting an international conference in Albuquerque, New Mexico. My subject, in part, focused on our attitude during periods of frustration, disappointment, and detours. I specifically stated that we should accept the detour in order to position ourself for a movement beyond the challenge.

Shortly after the presentation, I was approached by a very nice gentleman who inquired: "In reference to your

Traveling By Detour!

model for dealing with detours, would you mind if I exchanged the verb 'acknowledge' for the verb 'accept?'"

He continued, "I have Parkinson's Disease and I am willing to acknowledge it's presence, but I certainly do not want to accept it." I understood his point, but I have no problem with either "accept" or "acknowledge."

Acceptance Looks More Like Acknowledgement Than Acquiescence

The traveling by detour questions at this point are: "When I face a significant detour, do I accept it as a step in my response process, or do I flatly ignore or avoid it?" "Is my acceptance 'the continuation of a beginning?'" Or, "is my acceptance 'an ending?'"

By "accept," I do not mean acquiesce, give into, settle or submit. I do not mean to say: "I accept this detour; this is the way it is, I must simply live with it." I do not mean to say: "Alright, I accept it; the door for future growth is closed."

By "accept your detour," I mean "recognize" - yes, acknowledge. I do mean to say: "I accept this. This is the way it now is. Now, what do I do?" This genre of acceptance is not a dead-end acquiescence, it is a front-end invitation into the pursuit of response.

Living with Struggle and Surprise

It Is a Battle

This breed of acceptance may initially lead you to feel "sufficiently uncomfortable." But this surpasses mere denial as it states: "I do not like the way this is. I wish it had not happened. But here it is, I must deal with it."

To feel "sufficiently uncomfortable" is to recognize the tension between acceptance and denial. Sitting in the doctor's office, I often sense a "warring within" where acceptance and denial are fighting each other.

After many visits (certainly not every visit), I leave honoring acceptance and battling denial. Acceptance is the preferred option because it is a critical step in my living with struggle and surprise. At point of head and heart, and on most days, I celebrate the superiority of acceptance over denial.

This has never been an easy battle for me. Some have suggested that I need not have to try so hard at the task of a positive acceptance. The fact is: I do have to battle!

Parking, with No Exit

Acceptance contributes to a continuum that begins with anticipation and concludes with appreciation. Denial results in a problematic standing-still. A rebuff against reality can lead to a troublesome "parking - with no exit." Acceptance, for me, resembles an open door whereas denial makes me think of a closed door.

Traveling By Detour!

Stagnation at Best, Reversal at Worse

Acceptance, even when it emerges out from a crucible of struggle, can lead to things getting better. Denial can result in confusion, complication, and delayed medical treatment.

Acceptance of a detour can facilitate a meaningful struggle, even pleasant surprises. Denial thwarts any meaning within struggle and strangles pleasant surprises.

Denial, for me, is extremely destructive. It looks like procrastination, postponement, and an inevitable prolongation of deep frustration. Denial, at its best, resembles stagnation. Denial at its worse looks like reversal.

Denial equals my prison cell; acceptance equals another positive step in my growth cycle. When mania is battling against and within me, denial fuels the fury. Acceptance sets the stage for an "I need help."

Denial breathes that which is impeding; acceptance can result in an empowering. Denial inflicts heaps of hurt on others. Acceptance can intensify relief.

Denial reveals a self-centeredness that is reflected in a first-person emphasis (I, me, my, mine). Acceptance does account for the fact that denial hurts not only self, but others.

Denial is cocky, arrogant, and ultimately self-centered when it continually refuses to consider its impact upon others. In a very real sense, acceptance is actually unselfish.

Living with Struggle and Surprise

A Common Denominator

Denial and acceptance do have something in common. They are both choice-related. Denial, from my perspective, is a choice; so is acceptance.

Denial wants me to succumb to trickery. Denial wants me to think that I have no choice in the matter. But I do have a choice in the matter. I possess the ultimate choice.

My battle is against my tendency to sublimate any responsibility for my own wellness path. I must constantly remind myself that I am crafted as a choice-person.

My Heavenly Father blessed me with the capacity to choose. When I choose to deny the power of detours and struggles within my life, I choose to degregate my God-given capacity in a fashion that equals poor stewardship.

I know in my heart that I must be a good steward of all that He has given me - that includes the capacity to choose wisely. Thanks be to Him for forgiving me when I choose denial over acceptance. Thanks also be to Him for blessing me with courage and strength when I do choose the acceptance route: "This is the way it now is, now this is what I must do!"

~

Analysis, Not Retreat

*"Millions saw the apple fall, but Newton
is the one who asked why."*
Bernard Baruch

*"The important thing is not to stop questioning...
Never lose a holy curiosity."*
Albert Einstein

*"My heroes are the ones who survived doing it wrong,
who made mistakes, but recovered from them."*
Bono

*"What we call failure is not the falling down,
but the staying down."*
Mary Pickford

"The unexamined life is hardly worth living."
Socrates

~

A detour analyzed is less destructive than a detour unaddressed. Learning more about my detours/diseases has been helpful, blessing me with both hope and surprises resulting in a fuller life. I am grateful for step number three in my structure model 5A - Analysis.

Traveling By Detour!

What'll Ya Have?

The essence of this mile marker finds its birth place in a very famous restaurant located here in Georgia. The name of this restaurant is The Varsity.

The Varsity is known as the world's largest drive-in restaurant. The original Varsity opened in 1928.

The location in downtown Atlanta spans more than two acres. When the Georgia Tech Yellow Jackets are engaged in a home game, over 30,000 people visit The Varsity.

Daily, the varsity produces: Two miles of hot dogs, a ton of onions, 2500 pounds of potatoes, 5000 fried pies and 300 gallons of chili. All are made from scratch.

The Varsity now has several locations. Two landmark locations are near the Georgia Tech campus in Atlanta, and close to the University of Georgia in Athens.

As interesting as is all of the above data, you can ask Georgians what comes into their mind when they think of The Varsity, one answer will surface repeatedly. The answer equals the phrase that is uttered tens of thousands of times on any given weekend.

Upon entering this delightful restaurant, you will hear, resonating from behind the order counters, an incessant **"What'll ya have?"** This is The Varsity's way of asking for your order: Chilli Dog, Double Chilli Cheese Burger, Onion Rings, Fried Pies, etc.

Living with Struggle and Surprise

The analysis portion of my model for traveling by detour is grounded in three questions. Simply worded, I refer to this as my "What? Why? How?" method of analyzing.

This method begins with "What do you (I) have?" In Varsity terminology, this sounds like "What'll ya have?"

An Agenda for Growth

For many years, I have assisted my clients and audiences in developing their own personal Agenda for Growth. This Agenda for Growth is grounded in strength sculpting and weakness chiseling.

Personally, this format has helped me live with struggle and surprise. My own Agenda for Growth, the fulcrum of my analysis phase of the Model 5A, equals: What do you have? What do you want in its place? Why do you not now have what you want? What do you need to do to get what you want?

This can be worded another way. What can I learn from this detour? Why is learning important at this point? How can I implement what I have learned? If you look closely, the above will look like: Description, diagnosis, prescription.

It has proven helpful for me to isolate my detours for purposes of examination. By setting them aside, I can pursue a cause of a certain situation. I can also develop courses of action or response.

Anticipation set the stage. Acceptance open the curtain. Now Analysis is on stage - front and center!

The Big Two

As a college professor in the field of public speaking for more than a decade, I taught my students a fundamental principle. I told them that their speech would not fly within them, nor out from them, if the content could not stand on two legs: Outline and meat on bones.

The meat on bones is technically referred to as expository supporting material. The meat on bones would include illustrations, narratives, statistics, and examples.

Basically, the students needed to think in two's: Bones, and meat on bones. I encouraged them to utilize one particular "meat on bone approach." I stressed to them the importance of supporting their points with personal examples.

At this point in *Traveling By Detour! Living with Struggle and Surprise,* I want to share two examples of how I have used my "What do you have?" model. One example is Obsessive-Compulsive Disorder. It looks like an extreme anxiety, a ritual of checking, and thoughts that re-surface, without invitation, and then refuse to leave. I repeatedly choose to give them the power to rule over me.

The other example is Bipolar Disorder. It looks like an up and down swing of moods (unpredictable), and a lateral lock of depression where a dark heavy curtain hangs over me for a lengthy period of time. It can also look like a lateral lock in the "up" mode (hyperactivity and excessive spending).

Living with Struggle and Surprise

My psychiatrist/therapist has made it very clear to me that my condition would be easier for her to treat and less difficult upon me if I had one illness, not two. That is not my lot.

The paragraphs that follow will "example" how analysis in general, and "What do you have?" thinking in particular, have serviced my journey at the point of struggle and surprise.

Surprise

In the paragraphs that follow in this mile marker, "Analysis, Not Retreat," I will ask the key questions that lead me toward the analysis-option, not the retreat-response. It is important to note that, at this writing, I feel, with an unabashed affirmation, that this phase of the model continues to work for me. My surprise has been that it has worked so effectively.

When I think to ask the questions that follow, and when I implement the answers that surface, I stack the odds in my favor. I do not do this all the time. I fail on many occasions to follow my own model.

Another Surprise

I am not the only one who has observed my reluctance to stick to my own words. I smile even now when I think about what one of the children said years ago.

Traveling By Detour!

He was reading a book and seemed intrigued. After awhile he put down the book and blurted, "Mom, this is good, Dad should read this." It was a book that I had written.

It is now time for us to experience the questions at work at the point of Obsessive-Compulsive Disorder. Read well!

What Do You Have?
Obsessive-Compulsive Disorder

I have Obsessive-Compulsive Disorder. I did not choose it. I certainly have, however, chosen to complicate it. It is, to a large degree, a concoction of my chemistry and my experiences. It looks like this: Anxiety, unwanted thoughts that enter and will not leave, an incessant checking, a ritual of repetition, and a dominance over me that aggravates the hell out of me. I do not like this Obsessive-Compulsive Disorder.

My Non-verbal Stuttering

It is both interesting and ironic that, while I write this mile marker, I am engaged in a war. I am battling an actual mumbling or stuttering challenge that is either related to the medicines I take or to essential tremor.

It is intriguing to me that this challenge is not problematic, when I speak in public. My doctors indicate that it is my adrenaline that diffuses any mumbling or stuttering during the presentation.

Living with Struggle and Surprise

When I apply my, "What do you have?" Agenda for Growth model to my Obsessive-Compulsive Disorder, I discover something interesting. To a small degree, it does affect what I say. To a much larger degree, however, my Obsessive-Compulsive Disorder equals a "non-verbal" stuttering.

I equate non-verbal stuttering with "getting stuck" at the point of anxiety, horrific thoughts that enter my mind and will not leave, and an incessant checking. I associate non-verbal stuttering with repetitive activities that accomplish absolutely nothing. I identify non-verbal stuttering with "A being 'caught' at the point of worry," and a trap within the moment that endures for hours, even days.

What Do You Want in Its Place?

I want peace. I recognize that no one is normal. I would like to approach a standard of attitude and behavior that appears to be so familiar to others, but alien to me.

I do not expect perfect peace. I just want a lot more than I now have. I do not expect the non-verbal stuttering to totally evaporate.

I would like to see Obsessive-Compulsive Disorder have less power over me. I want to see my family and friends impacted less by an illness that belongs to me.

I want to feel much better, worry less, and begin to minimize those unwanted-thought-visitors. I do not expect to get well. I just want to get better!

Traveling By Detour!

Why Do You Not Have What You Want?

The first reason why I do not have what I want is, of course, the disease. I do not want Obsessive-Compulsive Disorder: The non-verbal stuttering, the unwanted recurring thoughts, the anxiety.

A second reason why I do not have what I want is that I do things that aggravate and complicate my illness. I cheat with caffeine and chocolate and refuse to follow the prescription instructions. I fail to follow the agreed upon response that I had with my psychiatrist/therapist and choose to watch television programs that enhance my obsession or depression. I refuse to practice meditation. I exhibit a half-hearted commitment to reading the books that have been recommended.

What Do You Need to Do to Get What You Want?

Stop cheating with sips of caffeine and tiny pieces of chocolate. Stop rationalizing my difficulty with following the prescription instructions. Cease using changes in time zones as an excuse. Take the medication as instructed - dosage and time.

Follow procedures as suggested by my psychiatrist/therapist. Be selective at the point of the programs I watch. Stop falling asleep during meditation. Read helpful books on the subject of Obsessive-Compulsive Disorder.

Living with Struggle and Surprise

There Is Power in Redundancy

The questions in this next session will be identical to the questions posed at the point of Obsessive-Compulsive Disorder. In most cases, the answers will vary only slightly.

Redundancy will prove helpful. I have seen repetition at work in both my presentations and in my books. I recognize, with an unabashed surety, that a modicum of superfluous emphasis is, not only helpful, but required if I am to stick to my model.

What Do You Have?
Bipolar Disorder

Bipolar Disorder equals a continuing illness that includes lengthy and radical mood-changes. A person who endures Bipolar Disorder will battle both highs (mania) and lows (depression).

The dark and heavy curtain hanging over me can present itself as a lateral lock of depression. The "down" will overpower the even-keeled and the "up."

Episodes of mania (the high) will curse me (and those around me) with "an out-of-control" state. On occasion I will be unaware that I am in such a state. My mania impacts others (family, friends, and even those with whom I am unacquainted) in the form of rudeness and irritability.

Traveling By Detour!

The previous paragraphs were detail in nature by intent, not by accident. I wanted to indicate the piling up, or the heap upon heap, that equals a persistent battle against depression and mania.

The "Up and Down" and the Lateral Lock

For the sake of emphasis, let me address again that Bipolar Disorder for me is not only an "up and down" unpredictable mood swing. That would prove challenging enough.

On occasion, the "down" mode (depression) seems to last much longer than the "up" mode (mania). On other occasions, extended periods of mania have dominated my life. I am not always aware of this domination.

The highs and lows are different for each person with this diagnosis. Some experience more frequent episodes of mania than depression.

What Do You Want in Its Place?

I want some relief. I do not expect a relief that is permanent. I want more breathing room, more relaxed moments. I prefer slots of time "where Stephen is all that Stephen can be at points of compassion, competency, and creativity." (I do recognize that there is a front-side to my illnesses that can enhance, to a degree, my creativity and my performance at work.)

Living with Struggle and Surprise

I would appreciate fewer mood swings and more warning. I would like to experience a less powerful "lateral lock" with lows (depression) and with highs (mania).

Why Do You Not Have What You Want?

The first reason why I do not have what I want is the illness. I do not want Bipolar Disorder: The mood swings, the lateral lock, the intensive and excessive behavior, the mania, and the rapidly changing ideas.

A second reason why I do not have what I want is that I do things that aggravate and complicate my illness: A refusing to follow the prescription instructions, failing to follow the agreed upon response that I had with my psychiatrist/therapist, a refusal to practice meditation, and a half-hearted commitment to reading the books that have been recommended.

I do not want an irritability and rudeness that often extends out from my illness. I want to treat my family, friends, and strangers with a sense of warmth and compassion.

What Do You Need to Do to Get What You Want?

Stop rationalizing a difficulty with following the prescription instructions because of changes in time zone. Take the medication as instructed - dosage and time. Follow procedures as suggested by my psychiatrist/therapist. Stop falling asleep during meditation. Read helpful books on the subject of Bipolar Disorder.

Description, Diagnosis, Prescription

The composite of analysis equals a bonding between description (the What?), diagnosis (the Why?), and prescription (the How?). This composite breaks down into four key questions. These four questions have served as the nucleus of this mile marker.

The analysis of "Description, Diagnosis, Prescription" is borrowed from medical verbiage. This presents us with yet another occasion to emphasize that I am not a doctor of psychiatry. The verbiage is simply an analogy or an illustration. If you wrestle with either of these disorders, or both of them, I strongly encourage you to seek professional help. Professional help, in no way, is the purpose of this book. This is only my journey, my traveling by detour.

Analysis Versus Retreat

Retreat kills the model. Anticipation and acceptance serve no purpose if they are not followed by analysis.

You can anticipate the detours in your life and note that anticipation lessens their sting. You can accept the detours in your life - "accept" not as a blind acquiescence, but "accept" as "This is they way it now is. Now, what do I need to do?"

Your anticipation and your acceptance will serve as nothing but folly, or time wasted, if you choose to allow retreat to surface as victor. It is your choice.

Analysis, on the other hand, equals the dividends that extend from the investment of anticipation and acceptance. Retreat equals a closed door, analysis equals an open door. Retreat can lead to further despair, analysis births hope.

While retreat stops the construction-process of the Model 5A, analysis supports and fuels the model. If retreat blocks application and appreciation from entering the picture, analysis invites and welcomes both.

Retreat can make a farce out of the investment of my time of struggle, my psychiatrist/therapist's time, and the support of my family. Analysis can create a force that validates my time of struggle, my psychiatrist/therapist's time, and the support of my family.

Surprise

Analysis does not steal my energy; it blesses me with inertia. While analysis certainly can be fatiguing, and even painful, for the most part, it excites me.

Time has taught me that analysis is very helpful. This gives me hope. Year after year, analysis has proven worth every moment I invested in it.

There have been many instances where analysis failed me, or where I failed it. I am sure that occasional disappointment will continue.

But this I do know, analysis sets the stage for something very important. Analysis invites and welcomes acceptance.

~

Application, Not Irrelevance

*"Creativity is the ability to introduce order
into the randomness of nature."*
Eric Hoffer

"If only I may grow: firmer, simpler - quieter, warmer."
Dag Hammarskjöld

"The way to get started is to quit talking and begin doing."
Walt Disney

*"Start by doing what is necessary, then what's possible,
and suddenly, you are doing the impossible."*
St. Francis of Assisi

*"The dictionary is the only place that
success comes before work."*
Vince Lombardi

~

A student reads the required reading; he studies the thorough notes taken in class. He becomes so familiar with the data, and all relevant processes, that he reaches the point of full retention.

The moment of the test arrives. The student takes the test. He refuses to utilize the information that he has studied.

Traveling By Detour!

The student receives an "F" on the test. He does learn something, however. He learns the rule of application.

A farmer plants forty-two rows of Silver Queen corn. The gentleman has been a farmer most of his life. His years with growing this marvelous Silver Queen corn have taught him the necessity for the following: 1) Commercial or organic fertilizer, 2) watering, 3) "working the ground," and 4) full sunlight. He knows that it takes all four to grow a stellar crop.

This spring, for some reason, perhaps as a test, he violates all of the four necessities. There is no fertilizer. He refuses to water. There is no "working the ground." He plants the seeds in the shade. He knows better, but refuses to apply what he knows.

The resulting crop is frail and never moves beyond a flimsy-stalk phase. He learns never to try this again. And, he learns something else - the rule of application.

The football team practices all summer long "the two minute drill." The first game arrives. With two minutes to go, the game is tied. This team is on their own twenty. They are eighty yards away from a touch-down.

The clock holds only forty-five seconds. The team falls apart, fails to secure one first-down. They knew what to do, but they forgot something. They forgot the rule of application.

The Christian who learns the power of forgiveness, but cannot move beyond grudge-holding, should learn this rule. The teenager who seeks to drive, while doing something else, but knows better, should learn this rule.

Living with Struggle and Surprise

The student, the farmer, the football team, the Christian, and the teenage driver have something in common. They have failed to apply what they knew.

Form Minus Force Equals Farce

As you and I travel by detour, as we wrestle with both struggle and surprise, we must never forget that application is the fulcrum of Structure Model 5A. This must find a permanent place of residence within our inner-life cupboard.

All the work we have invested at the points of anticipation, acceptance, and analysis is for naught - void application. Minus application, the Structure Model 5A equals irrelevance. Application equals the proof of the process.

As I speak across the country and seas, I am constantly battling what I understand as a national trend. I believe, with full conviction, that I do not contribute to the trend. I also believe that other keynote speakers, trainers and presenters, for the most part, do not serve as the root of this national trend. It is, however, a sobering thought.

Close to seventy percent of the knowledge presented, and supposedly absorbed by keynote or seminar participants, evaporates within approximately one week. The rule of application never had a chance to take root at the point of head and heart within the participants. The problem lies within the participants and their unwillingness, or inability, to apply what they have learned.

Traveling By Detour!

Information Minus Implementation Equals Irritation

The information provided by anticipation, acceptance, and analysis might as well be an empty vessel if it does not bring implementation. It is not enough to plan, to accept the facts, and to analyze the situation. If application does not come to life, then what you have is an irritating irrelevance.

Intention will never get it done. "Meaning well" on its own accomplishes nothing. "Getting around to it" never seems to "get around to it."

Attitude will fall short. Behavior is required. Knowledge falls short of wisdom when behavior does not follow on the heels of appropriate attitude.

It is my experience that where there is no application, there is no growth. I not only fail to advance; I feel as if I am not even in the game.

Surprise

When I choose (remember it is all about choice) application over retreat, I progress. When I bless attitude with behavior, and the idea with the action, I move forward. When I value application, I diffuse irrelevance.

The mantra with which I seek to live is one word. It is a very powerful word.

Apply! Apply!! Apply!!!

~

Appreciation, Not a Mere Positive Attitude

"He is a wise man who does not grieve for the things which he has not, but rejoices for those which he has."
Epictetus

"No one is as capable as gratitude as one who has emerged from the kingdom of night."
Elie Wiesel

"Reflect upon your present blessings, of which every man has plenty; not on your past misfortunes of which all men have some."
Charles Dickens

"If you don't give a bit of yourself to someone else, you are a failure."
Robert Mastruzzi

~

Surprise

You may notice that this is the first time a sub-heading has been utilized at starting point of a mile marker. I have done this for a reason. I am more excited about this mile marker than any other segment in *Traveling By Detour!*

Traveling By Detour!

It is certainly not the most important mile marker. I stated in the previous segment that the very fulcrum of the book is mile marker fourteen: Application. This section on appreciation or gratitude does hold a stellar position in my heart. This part of the book will reveal the most significant surprise I have encountered in traveling by detour.

The Front-End, Not Merely the Back-End

Prior to the last ten years, I held no comprehension that gratitude could be so powerful. Indeed, my appreciation for gratitude has escalated within recent years. When I am inclined to visit my pity pot, and when I actually touch the seat of the pot, gratitude kicks me off.

I need to make it very clear that I do not appreciate my detours. There is nothing that I appreciate about Obsessive-Compulsive Disorder or Bipolar Disorder. What I do appreciate is what I have learned from traveling by detour.

One of the main things I have learned is this: Gratitude resides not only on the "back-end" of "someone or something" wonderful happening. Gratitude lives also on the "front-end" - providing both an initiative and a rudder that equals inspiration. "I am grateful" - and something wonderful happens.

Gratitude for the blessings of medicine, therapy, and support have helped to keep me going. Although I have not always taken advantage of my blessings, reflection reveals their power within my life.

Living with Struggle and Surprise

Gratitude on the "front-end" also has significance within my inner-life cupboard. Time and again, I have experienced gratitude "freeing me up" to share my struggle in front of hundreds of thousands of people.

Keynote after keynote, workshop after workshop, I have been grateful for hundreds who have approached me. I have a deep spirit of gratitude for the opportunity they gave me on the "front-end" to encourage and support them.

In specific terms, I am grateful for three particular things: 1) My Heavenly Father, His Son, and His Holy Spirit, 2) the support of my family, friends, and clients, and 3) the power behind authentic vulnerability.

Both Life-Jacket and Diving-Board

As I have struggled with Obsessive-Compulsive Disorder and Bipolar Disorder for most of my life, knowingly for almost twenty years, I have experienced gratitude as a marvelous "life-jacket." I am grateful for all the people who have been there for me, and are there for me. But gratitude has proven to be much more than a "life-jacket." This equals the root of my big surprise.

I fully recognize that it is normally inappropriate to jump off of a "diving-board" with a "life-jacket" - except for unusual situations that would require supervision. However, my big surprise transcends gratitude as "life-jacket" and embraces gratitude as "diving-board."

Traveling By Detour!

With a spirit of gratitude on the "front-end," I have been able to "springboard" out from struggle time and again. When struggle reappears, I have been able to retrieve an encouraging spirit of gratitude.

That retrieval has enabled me to move off the launching pad. It has also gifted me with both initiative and a rudder.

Both an Attitude and a Behavior

Gratitude on the "back-end" has served as response. Gratitude on the "front-end" has been much more than an attitudenal response for me; it has also served as a behavioral reaction. Worded another way, gratitude has become not merely what I feel or think. Gratitude has become much larger than it used to be - transcending feeling and equaling behavior.

My stellar surprise is this: I am grateful for an ability to cope. I am also grateful for the capacity to utilize, or leverage my "where I have been" to encourage myself and others.

I will never again think of gratitude only in "back-end" terms. I am grateful for making it through very long nights. My gratitude blesses me with power for future challenges. There is power within gratitude. It is more than a feeling. I experience this as fact.

I believe in the power of gratitude on the "front-end." My belief is firm enough as to create within me a desire to share my belief and my experience as often as I can.

Living with Struggle and Surprise

Gratitude Can Help Change a Life

Gratitude will never give all it wants to as long as you confine it to "attitude." Gratitude has more to offer than feeling, belief, or opinion.

Gratitude holds enough potency to help you change your life. But gratitude will only help you if you choose to allow it. Once again, the choice lies within you.

With all the vigor that I can muster, I suggest that gratitude is therapeutic in nature. A spirit of appreciation has enabled me to bounce beyond my bruises, to get off of my pity pot.

Gratitude has been of a remarkable service to my growth-journey. I sincerely encourage you to ponder how gratitude might service your journey as well.

The critical point to believe and to practice is this: Do not hold gratitude back by limiting it to the "back-end" response-mode. Celebrate how it can help you on the "front-end." Let gratitude loose! Let it loose!!

~

Our Capacity to Sputter

*"I have had more trouble with myself than
with any other man I've met."*
Dwight Moody

*"Enduring setbacks while maintaining the ability to show others
the way to go forward is a true test of leadership."*
Nitin Nohria

*"God will not look you over for medals, degrees,
or diplomas, but for scars."*
Elbert Hubbard

"'Detourlessness' is an illusion!"
SMG

~

I own a 1977 truck. It is big and blue. My friends call it ugly. I only drive it about every three months. When I crank it, there is an invariable sputter, a mechanical stammering that indicates the engine's inconsistency at the point of full power.

I can identify with my big, blue truck because I am persistently out of touch with constancy. I sputter my way toward new starts day after day. I am incessantly "beginning again."

My movements toward growth are interrupted with distractions, both internal and external. My struggling with detours resembles the stock market where "the dip" is inevitable. My battle is ongoing. Distractions are a persistent piece of the Obsessive-Compulsive Disorder.

Traveling By Detour!

Cyclical, Not Linear

A heart attack in 2005, a subsequent open heart surgery with four bypasses, caught my attention in a significant fashion. The heart attack, the surgery, and my journey toward recovery has reinforced what I already knew. When it comes to growth within individuals, we have a capacity to sputter!

My heart recovery did not unfold without hiccups - literally and figuratively. Repeatedly, I stood in my way! Progress in diet would establish itself, until I chose minor variances - then major diversions - then to restart! Exercise would begin to pay dividends, until I wavered - then chose to halt - then chose to begin again.

Just as with my journey toward a recovery within my heart (start, stop, re-start), so does the personal growth journey unfurl. Whether the struggle is against procrastination or impatience, with Obsessive-Compulsive Disorder or Bipolar Disorder, there is the likelihood of a stumbling.

If the challenge is weight-loss, within relationships or disappointments, growth is not linear in nature. Growth is cyclical at its very core. It does not unfold void of interruptions, distractions, and a robust sputtering at the point of initiative and energy.

Personal growth is never easy!

Living with Struggle and Surprise

Growth: Model 6R

Because personal growth is so difficult, and because I know detours are often at every corner, it is essential to be equipped for the journey. When there are many bumps as I seek to bring to life Anticipation, Acceptance, Analysis, Application and Appreciation, I turn to this process.

I encourage you to highlight this process in your book. It will be helpful to present this process in smaller increments. Believe me, you will experience each element as you learn how to live with struggle and surprise. Life is all about this - learning to deal with situations with which we are presented.

These six elements are sequential. They build upon each other. This is an important concept to understand.

Let me emphasize again that this concept is cyclical at its core. Element number six is designed to lead you back to element number one.

Worded another way, this is a process that is always beginning again. It is, in one manner, a living organism for traveling by detour.

These six elements are never to be discarded. They are to be valued. You have every right to be excited about what is to follow. It will service your journey as you wrestle with your capacity to sputter.

We will now explore: Recognition, Resolution, Response, Reneging, Regression, Re-visitation!

Recognition

*"You must accept responsibility for your actions,
but not the credit for your achievements."*
Denis Waitley

*"You cannot challenge yourself until you
recognize the challenge."*
SMG

~

I recognize what the challenge is: "I am traveling by a detour. I am not doing very well. I want to do better. I have much work to do."

Recognition is channeled to overpower denial! There are many challenges that could fall into the recognition area: Impatience, procrastination, an intense fear about speaking in public, a weight issue, and a grudge holding issue.

Other possible challenges that could mandate recognition are an intense physical examination and a required fresh approach to diet and exercise. Additional challenges could equal a battle against low self-esteem (one of my battles) and a war against substance abuse.

The purpose of this book is certainly not to suggest that your challenge, and/or the challenge of a family member, is Obsessive-Compulsive Disorder and Bipolar Disorder. I do recognize, however, that Obsessive-Compulsive Disorder or Bipolar Disorder may be the precise challenge you face. This observation is based on the fact that we are receiving a significant number of advance orders for *Traveling By Detour!* These orders have come immediately after my presentation when I referred to my struggle and the soon-to-be released book.

Sophie Had It Right, and She Was Cool

Sophie Tucker was born on January 13, 1884 and passed away on February 9, 1966. She was heralded as a vaudeville entertainer and was known as the last of the "Last of the Red Hot Mamas."

My encounter with Ms. Tucker was brief. It occurred while I was at the Clayton Motor Lodge in Clayton, Georgia. I was taking a weekend jaunt with my parents and sister. The date was circa 1960. This was just a few years before Ms. Tucker's passing.

I would love to say that I met her in person. I came to know Ms. Tucker by way of the Ed Sullivan Show. I was blessed to watch while in Clayton. For some reason, the moment has found permanent residence in my memory-bank.

I only remember one phrase in the song that she sang. I do not even know the title of the song. All I remember is the phrase: "Take the first step and then go all the way."

Recognition is the first step in facing your challenge! Personal growth, at the point of your challenge requires a start!

Traveling By Detour!

Resolution

"Always bear in mind that your own resolution to succeed is more important than any one thing."
Abraham Lincoln

"We need the positive virtues of resolution, of courage, of indomitable will."
Theodore Roosevelt

"Never forget that it is the spirit with which you endow your work that makes it useful or futile."
Adelaide Hasse

~

On the hills of recognition comes the will, the resolving to do something about the situation. Circumstances will marry choices to mold the Resolution.

I understand resolution as an internal mandate, a surety and clarity of purpose. It is also the determination to adhere to both the mandate and the purpose.

Resolution is attitude. It has to do with feelings, not behavior. It is related to an outlook, not an action.

Our capacity to sputter, to hem and haw, to falter time and again, will never diminish unless we bring something special and specific to task. That something special is a resolution.

When our traveling by detour births a recognition challenge, we must make a promise to ourselves. "Resolve!"

Living with Struggle and Surprise

Response

"You've got to get to the stage in life where going for it is more important than winning or losing."
Arthur Ashe

"Nothing will work unless you do."
Maya Angelou

"Accountability breeds response-ability."
Stephen R. Covey

~

What becomes the meat on the bones of resolution is a response that equals a behavior. When "I am determined to take action" becomes "I take action," that is Response.

Intent alone will not fuel the difficult process of personal growth. Neither will accident automatically feed the growth cycle. Personal growth requires more than either intent or accident. It requires a response.

When I sputter, when I stammer and stumble, it is often because I do not make it to the response stage. I must be accountable at this point.

I cannot pass the blame onto my "army of allies" or to my "arsenal of resources." Where there is no response, I am at fault. If I authentically want to service my journey, I must move beyond recognition of a particular, and often daunting challenge. I must transcend an attitudinal resolving.

I must respond with a plan of action!

Reneging

"If you falter, and give up, you will lose the power of keeping any resolution, and will regret it all your life."
Abraham Lincoln

"Prosperity is a great teacher; adversity a greater."
William Hazlitt

"Reneging is inevitable."
SMG

~

To renege is "to go back on." To violate a promise to one's self equals a Reneging. Reneging is an attitude, not a behavior. Whereas "resolve" is a positive attitude, "reneging" is negative.

Resolve sets the stage for a continuation of the difficult process of personal growth. Reneging breaks down the stage, or a part of it.

There is a critical point to be made at this juncture of *Traveling By Detour! Living with Struggle and Surprise.* Reneging need not be all powerful. It does not have to equal a closing of the door of personal growth.

It is a "slow down." I encourage you to prepare yourself for it. A failure to anticipate an attitudinal "backing off" or "promise-breaking" will prove to be a crucial error.

By factoring the expectation of reneging into your personal growth equation, it need not equal a costly shock.

Living with Struggle and Surprise

Regression

"The credit belongs to the man who is actually in the arena, whose face is marred by dust and sweat and blood, who strives valiantly, who errs and comes short again and again..."
Theodore Roosevelt

"Regression is to reneging, as response is to resolution."
SMG

~

If response is the extension of resolution, then regression is the result of reneging. The violation of an appropriate response equals a reneging.

The reneging leads to a sputtering, perhaps even a stalling. Reneging eventually takes consequence in the form of Regression.

Just as reneging is to be anticipated, so is regression. As you travel the difficult journey that equals personal growth, there will be detours. One of your detours will look like regression - a moving backwards, downhill.

Regression pushes the foot a little more firmly on the brakes of personal growth. It impedes the progress.

Regression, however, is not exclusively negative at its core. Regression can be a grand tutor.

We can learn from our "where we have been." Our past performance need not be indicative of future results.

It will be appropriate to spend some time in the area of regression that may be categorized as mistakes. We can profit here.

Traveling By Detour!

On Mistakes

One of my first presentations this year was an event that I routinely anticipate with much vigor: The Annual Diverse Power Leadership Institute for High School Students in LaGrange, Georgia.

We started this venture in 2005. It has become a stellar program. This is in large part because of the vision and community-focus of Diverse Power, and because of the principals and students who represent the seven schools involved.

An issue that surfaced this year, arising out from both my comments and the students' Just Like Thinking exercises, was grounded in the relationship between leadership and mistakes. I admit that I was somewhat shocked when I asked the student-participants to share some nuggets they had learned thus far in the day.

Routinely, their comments centered on how we can learn from our mistakes. Of course, the students were correct - we can indeed profit from "our where we have been - even if that equals mistakes."

However, due to the intensity and frequency of the students' responses, I felt the need to revisit the issue of detours and mistakes later in the day. I shared with these young leaders two keeper-thoughts that I choose to restate.

Before a re-stating, let me make perfectly clear that my illness did not occur because of any mistakes I made. The mistakes I have made did not cause my illness, but they did (and do) complicate and intensify my illnesses.

Now let me share two fundamental thoughts on mistakes and our traveling by detour. Read well!

1) There are some mistakes that we just cannot make! Mistakes related to safety, legal issues, and certain confidentiality matters must not occur.

I remember hearing the reseachable Dr. Betty Segal, the former President of Kennesaw College in Marietta, Georgia refer to mistakes or errors as being either glass balls or rubber balls. In her marvelous analogy, the rubber balls (some mistakes) would bounce back and we could try again. The glass balls (other mistakes), once dropped, would not bounce back - leaving permanent, often drastic, consequences.

This anecdote remains within my head and heart after almost a quarter of a century. Caution: When dealing with glass balls, be very careful.

2) Other mistakes (less caustic ones) can actually serve as tutors. As we travel by detour, we can profit from our mistakes. Often, there is educational value within a mistake. Regression can teach us many beneficial lessons.

Responding to mistakes can look like this: 1) A mistake is acknowledged - forthrightly. 2) A mistake is corrected - promptly. 3) There is compensation - when appropriate.

Learning from our mistakes can involve three simple questions: 1) What went wrong? 2) Why did the mistake occur? 3) How can I modify and move beyond the mistake?

Traveling By Detour!

Re-visitation

"Never confuse a single defeat with a final defeat."
F. Scott Fitzgerald

*"When one door closes another door opens; but we so often
look so long and so regretfully open the closed door,
that we do not see the ones which open for us."*
Alexander Graham Bell

"Accomplishments will prove to be a journey, not a destination."
Dwight D. Eisenhower

~

Hopefully, regression becomes an "attention-getter." The "attention-getting" can lead to an "about face" and a "forward march."

A "forward march" is actually a revisit to recognition. It sets the stage of refueling the cycle of growth. This critical step (and first re-step) is arguably a crucial phrase of personal growth. It is Re-visitation.

Our capacity to sputter (to sporadically falter) need not perpetually fuel the "back-end" (regression). It can lead to the "front-end" (re-visitation).

Those who choose to re-visit personal growth are sending an important reminder our way. There is a viable alternative to perpetual sputtering.

Regression need not hault the process. Regression can lead to re-visitation.

Living with Struggle and Surprise

Re-visitors Are Welcome

By valuing and implementing the 6 R's (Recognition, Resolution, Response, Reneging, Regression, Re-visitation), we can actually learn to live with struggle and surprise. We need not stumble as much. Comprehending Re-visitation is critical!

Surprise

The essence of re-visitation is hope. It equals a huge second chance. Re-visitation is not the finish line. Re-visitation is a fresh start.

Re-visitation does not halt the process. It continues the process. A grand surprise is this: Re-visitation leads back to recognition, then to resolution, then to response.

As you travel by detour and as you live with struggle and surprise, you have every right to be excited about the hope that lies within re-visitation. Personal growth is difficult; re-visitation fascilitates the journey.

When you sputter, it is critical to remember an exciting and inviting truth. Re-visitors are welcome!

~

Diffuse the Beast

*"The acknowledgment of our weakness is the
first step in repairing our loss."*
Thomas Kempis

"Truth is always exciting. Speak it, then. Life is dull without it."
Pearl Buck

"Admission, not submission, stifles the adversary."
SMG

~

The setting was Delaware. Noon brought a lunch break during my presentation. A delightful lady approached, immediately addressing me with: "I just want to thank you for the way you began your presentation. It will help me more than you can imagine in dealing with a particular challenge I face."

I knew to which she was referring. And, I do expect it will prove helpful for her.

I remember the day well. For a reason which is more complicated than this mile marker will allow, I was experiencing a significant tremor on my left hand. The tremor has been my companion for a long time now, but on this day it was obviously angry with me.

Less than one minute into the presentation, I remember sharing: "Now the basic themes of the day will be: a) The Power of Perception over Reality, b) the Negative Nature of

Traveling By Detour!

Assumption, c) the Difference between Leadership and Management, d) Journey Servicing As a Fundamental Tenet of Nurturing, and e) the Reality of Traveling By Detour."

"Speaking of traveling by detour, that is what I am doing today. Those of you who are seated on the front rows will notice a testy tremor on my left hand.

It is complicated today by the medicines I am taking for another condition. I just wanted you to know what was going on down there at the point of my left hand."

With those few words, I had diffused the beast. "What they were thinking about the tremor" no longer held any power over me whatsoever.

It was no longer a case of "advantage: tremor." It was now a case of "advantage: Stephen." The admission led to the diffusing. The diffusing led to the advantage. Vulnerability gifted me with a victory over obsessive thoughts about the distracting nature of the tremor.

Let me share several examples where I have observed others diffusing their beasts. Their examples are encouraging!

How They Won Their Battles

The gentleman who sweats profusely when he speaks in public begins his presentation with: "Now I want to warn you. I am very passionate about this message. Part of my makeup is that when I get passionate about a subject, I begin to sweat. So please expect some sweating. It is just the way I am."

In my opinion, the gentleman not only diffused his

beast (his sweating and the potential power it held over him), he endeared himself to his audience. His vulnerability opened more doors than it closed.

A student approaches a teacher at the beginning of a semester: "Dr. Jones, I have attention deficit disorder. I am not seeking any excuses and take full responsibility for my grades. I see my doctor monthly and we think we have the situation under control."

"What I would appreciate is this: If you notice regression on my part, and suspect that I may not be aware of it, would you be so kind as to share your observation with me?" Beast diffused.

A Personal Example

For five plus years, I have been diffusing my beasts (Obsessive-Compulsive Disorder and Bipolar Disorder). After many years of struggle, I decided to be open with my audiences about my illnesses. I reached the conclusion that my vulnerability would serve two purposes.

On the first hand, it would help me. It would take pressure off of me. I would worry much less about how these illnesses were impacting my presentations.

In the second case, my vulnerability, what was an initial diffusing of the beasts, would help others. This is a significant piece of this book.

The concept of "diffusing beasts" and encouraging others is a powerful idea. It is so potent that it leads to our next

Traveling By Detour!

two mile markers: *A Different Slant on Making a Difference* and *Nurture Not Nature.*

Before moving to our next segment, I want to state that one specific book has assisted me at this point. The book is: *The Wounded Healer* by Henri J. M. Nouwen. It is a tremendous work. I highly recommend it.

Fundamentally, as I understand it, this book addresses two significant scriptural truthes: Jesus was wounded by our transgressions; we are healed by His stripes.

I recognize that I take much liberty with the title, but I use it as an important reminder. I think you and I can think and act as if we are lowercase wounded healers.

If you have gone through divorce, you can help service the journey of someone going through such a detour. If you are experiencing Obsessive-Compulsive Disorder and Bipolar Disorder, you can identify with and nurture the person traveling a similar detour.

When you diffuse the beast, you not only take pressure off of yourself, you may make a difference in another's life. Traveling by detour is facilitated when you service your (and their) journey by diffusing the beast.

~

A Different Slant on Making a Difference

"Hide not you talents, they for use were made.
What's a sun-dial in the shade?"
Benjamin Franklin

"A miracle is not that we do this work but
that we are happy to do it."
Mother Teresa

"It's easy to make a buck. It's a lot tougher to make a difference."
Tom Brokaw

"Making a positive difference in the lives of those
who travel by detour is a choice."
SMG

~

On the occasion of our executive assistant's graduation ceremony (with her receiving signal honors), I found myself revisiting my years as a college professor in the field of public speaking. The ceremony featured two speeches by graduating students.

There were two points of commonality in the presentations: Stellar delivery styles and similarity as to content. In each speech, the theme of "making a difference" was established.

Traveling By Detour!

The students sought to inspire their colleagues with language such as: "You have the potential to dream big, to reach your dreams, and to make a difference in our world." What was said was not only said well, it was true.

It is "what was not said" that I found intriguing. In fairness, at their age, I certainly would not have thought to have said "it." However, I am the beneficiary of bonus decades of observation and experience.

A different slant on the subject of "making a difference" equals several points (the "it") that I want to address.

Making a Difference on the Home Front and Out There

Before I share these observations, I would like to offer a hope. My hope is not only for those of us who travel with heavy detours. My hope is for those family members and friends who are perpetually affected by our traveling by detour. May the following be helpful as you seek to make a difference both within yourself and out from yourself, both on the home front and out there.

It is also necessary to emphasize that making a difference in the lives of other people is extremely therapeutic for those of us who travel by detour. Low self-esteem is serviced when eyes are taken off the self. Narcissistic behavior has less potency when we, with as much purity of motive as we can muster, seek to make a difference in the lives of others.

Making a Difference Is a Four-legged Stool

1) The effort to make a difference will not always be successful. Ultimately, this should not prove problematic because our internal mandates require a greater emphasis on a faithful effort than a guaranteed success.

Desiring to soar is not only worthwhile thinking; it is admirable thinking. It is the expectation of a perpetual success that creates a stumbling, not a soaring.

I attempted to make a difference in the lives of my students while I was teaching public speaking on the college level. On many occasions I was successful. Even now, twenty years later, I am still being thanked for the contribution I made to a person's life.

On other occasions, I made no difference. Perhaps the student "just did not get it" or I was totally ineffective. After several classes, I learned to anticipate a modicum of disappointment (the void of success).

This did not diminish my effort, nor did it impact my success. It did bless me at the point of the relationship between unrealistic expectations and the temptation to place too much pressure upon myself.

2) The effort to make a difference can be successful, but not apparent. Simply because you do not see the results, or fruits, of your labor at making a difference does not mean you were not successful. I personally believe that God blesses us with glimpses of instances where we do make a

difference - in part to keep us inspired. But in many cases, only He will know what a huge difference you make in the lives of many people.

I will never forget what one parent said to me at the conclusion of my time with a group of teenagers: "You have no idea, do you, as to the difference you have made in these young peoples' lives?" He was correct; I had no idea - successful, but not apparent.

3) The effort to make a difference can be successful, but not at the point you intended or expected. Bless yourself with some wiggle-room between your expectations and the actual results/outcomes.

The difference you intended may not be the difference that unfolded. Honor the difference you made, even if it is not the difference you intended.

I cannot count the times when corporate clients, upon the conclusion of my presentation on "What Do They See When They See You Coming?," approached me and shared something special with me. What they have said has serviced my journey in significant fashion.

"Stephen, I know you came here expecting to impact our corporate culture, and you have touched our team members at that point. But what I must tell you is your words were most helpful for me at the point of a struggling relationship I have with one of my children. I cannot thank you enough for the insight you gave me."

Living with Struggle and Surprise

These persons perpetually bless me with a beneficial insight into "making a difference." "The barometer for success need not be so rigid as to limit where success may unfold - successful, but not where expected."

4) The effort to make a difference is process, not event. In a "quick-fix" culture, the tendency is to expect "instant success." Differences are more likely to unfold out from "the crock pot" rather than "the deep fryer."

Routinely, "cooking the difference" takes time. The "taking time" part is facilitated once you learn to celebrate "incremental finished-ness." As you seek to make a difference, note with satisfaction your progress. Refuse to wait for destination-arrival. Celebrate your journey. Chunk your celebration down into little pieces.

I had tremendous difficulty starting my first book. Excuses overpowered incentives. Postponement out-positioned initiative. I found myself imagining the book not happening much more often than I found myself imagining the book happening.

Procrastination held the advantage - "until!" Until I learned to celebrate "incremental finished-ness," there was no book. Once I valued the process of writing a book, I actually reveled in the challenges.

The moment I learned to value the title, then the outline, I celebrated. When I completed a word, then a sentence, then a paragraph, and then a chapter, I celebrated.

Traveling By Detour!

A different slant on making a difference equals a four legged stool that you occupy at your approaching graduation ceremony: The effort to make a difference will not always be successful. The effort to make a difference can be successful, but not apparent. The effort to make a difference can be successful, but not at the point you intended or expected. The effort to make a difference is process, not event.

Graduation Time

Graduation equals an enigma. "Finished-ness" invites commencement. Accomplishment summons new challenges.

Definitions of "making a difference" flex with the benefit of experience and hindsight. The depth of the differences you make will be enhanced when you graduate to a different slant on "making a difference."

~

Nurture, Not Nature

*"Never let a problem to be solved become more
important than the person to be loved."*
Barbara Johnson

*"We've got this gift of love, but love is like a precious plant.
You can't just accept it and leave it in the cupboard or just think
it's going to get on by itself. You've got to keep watering it.
You've got to really look after it and nurture it."*
John Lennon

~

Two previous mile markers, *Our Capacity to Sputter* and *A Different Slant on Making a Difference* set the stage for an invitation. Think nurture, not nature.

I am the beneficiary of a very gifted wife who serves as the Executive Vice President of The Gower Group, Inc. as well as our office manager. Lynne excels at "thinking nurture, not nature." I am grateful for her talent at this point.

For almost fifteen years, our office has maintained a stellar relationship with the Work Program at our local high school, the Stephens County High School. We have benefited from a work force composed mainly of high school juniors and seniors.

These students have blessed us with remarkable computer techniques and with amazing interpersonal skills. They have brought a spirit of dedication that has touched my heart. Several have chosen to work with us well into their college years. Many return for personal visits.

Invariably, however, these students have initially approached us with a manner that appears constricted, excessively quiet, guarded, reserved beyond the norm. This may not be their real nature, but it has certainly been the nature they have exhibited during their first few weeks with us.

Our veteran team members think that my personality accounts for a large portion of our newcomers' timidity and nervousness. I recognize that my demeanor contributed, to a degree, to their feeling intimidated or overwhelmed.

Nevertheless, it is appropriate to state that these students have approached their initial interview and their first weeks with an attitude and a behavior that has exemplified a "camouflaging." I have felt, on a persistent basis, as if these students had much more to give than they initially revealed.

It was as if their nature was to camouflage their potential. Their exhibited nature equaled reluctance rather than initiative, a void of confidence rather than self-confidence. This revealed nature was holding them, and to a degree our company, captive to less than a maximized performance.

This is where my wife comes in. This is where she has been entering the scene for more than a decade. Her "entering the scene" has proven remarkably effective because she thinks nurture, not nature.

Her approach is never personality-obliteration or even personality-alteration. She takes a path instead that leads to personality-expression, even personality-enhancement.

For many years, I have observed Lynne transform an exhibited nature of timidity into a revealed nature of tenacity. The difference was in the "nurture."

Year after year, Lynne has massaged release into a spirit where there was reserve, even retreat. On many occasions, she has crafted a gem out from a stone. The difference was in the "nurture."

As a result of Lynne's skill at the point of nurture, many stellar developments have emerged within, and out from, those who work with us. An emphasis on inadequacy has been replaced with self-confidence first, then initiative.

Work that appeared to be chore, has become choice. "Obligation" had revealed itself as a predominant attitude, now it is "opportunity."

The counting of the weeks "until this is over" has been exchanged with "Can we arrange the schedule so I can work while going to college?"

Nurturing in the Midst of the Detour

You may be seeking ways to service the journey of other persons who travel with you, bringing to the path their own detours of challenge. Or, you may be searching for ways to service the journey of a particular loved one, trapped by heavy detour and deep struggle.

Traveling By Detour!

It will be helpful to understand nurturing as that which is not as simple as many of us have previously thought. Nurturing can prove to be complex.

1) It may begin as an attitude; but authentic nurturing will never remain in the attitudinal state. Genuine nurturing is much more than "giving a hoot" or "caring" or "feeling."

2) Ultimately, others respond to your behavior (they may not even know your attitudes). Nurturing will never occur if it is only an attitude you hold. Nurturing must look like a behavior that you exhibit.

3) If you are a nurturer who has been bumped and bruised, you may become a more effective nurturer. "When you have been there or somewhere like there," you will be more inclined to bring passion and insight to task.

4) The verbs "nurture" and "encourage" are similar in meaning. Neither is an "one-time-thing." Both are progressive or cyclical in nature.

5) Nurturing is reciprocal at the core. Often, what you send out bounces back toward you and catches you with a pleasant surprise.

6) The language of nurturing must be specific. The little word "because" will benefit you as you seek to nurture another: "Sally, you are doing a great job here because you are having to deal with several personal challenges while you are working. If you don't mind Sally, may I add this: 'The model you set for our team is exemplary. I think you are helping other team members without even knowing it.'"

7) Nurturing will not always seem to work. It may have more to do with them than with you. Consider encouraging another to seek professional help.

8) Nurturing can, on occasion, look more like receiving than giving. Remember: the capacity to receive from them can equal a great gift to them.

9) Appropriate laughter is often "a relaxer" or "a hinge" that helps you open the door to the point of understanding. Laugh at yourself, not them.

Many of us have a lot to work with at this point. Keep your humor clean. Laughter can help birth a nurturing environment. (Remember: There are occasions when laughter will be inappropriate.)

10) Nurturing can be rewarding. Making a difference can be remarkably meaningful and satisfying.

Think nurture, not nature!

~

Struggle Well

"Watch your thoughts; they become words. Watch your words; they become actions. Watch your actions; they become habits. Watch your habits; they become character. Watch your character; it becomes your destiny."
Frank Outlaw

"Turn your wounds into wisdom."
Oprah Winfrey

"A bouquet of surprise often emerges out from a crucible of struggle."
SMG

~

As we engage in our final mile marker of *Traveling By Detour! Living with Struggle and Surprise,* I have a confession. I have a history of having less difficulty with "hellos" and more difficulty with "goodbyes." However, that time is now approaching.

I will begin to conclude our time together with the following story. The event occurred in 2006.

I had just completed a presentation. I was approached by a gentleman whose comment has lodged permanently within my spirit and mind.

Now you must understand how unusual this is. Having given thousands of presentations, I have received hundreds of thousands of comments. His comment, stands above all others.

Traveling By Detour!

On this particular day, I was struggling with a plethora of detours. I was recouping from a heart attack, battling Obsessive-Compulsive Disorder and Bipolar Disorder, and even fighting my essential tremor.

As I mentioned in a previous mile marker, I choose to be open about my struggles, and my surprises. As I indicated earlier, there are several reasons that support this decision.

This day was no exception. At some point in the midst of a three hour presentation, I made a casual reference to my challenges and the Structure Model 5A (Anticipation, Acceptance, Analysis, Application, Appreciation).

The gentleman's words were succinct: "Mr. Gower, you suffer well!" I felt like I had to sit down. The two words, "struggle well," ministered to my soul.

My tears are easily accessible. I had to fight back them that day. In two words, the gentleman had summarized most of what I wanted to say in the book that I would write in 2007 (this book).

Its words equal the very fulcrum of these pages, the nexus of these thoughts, the core of the concepts. My hat is off to him. In my heart, I will be grateful to him.

Not only did he service my journey and massage my environment, he blessed me with an insight that will reside in my Precious File of thoughts. I feel better equipped to share with my audiences.

I hold both a spirit of confidence and competence because of his encouragement. I was truly blessed. My error was in not securing his address so that I could write a "thank you" note that was very specific. I would have had much to say to this fine gentleman.

"Sir, I know the capacity to receive can equal a grand gift. I hope you will respond to the fact that I 'receive' your statement more than you can imagine. I further hope that 'my receiving' will be a gift to you.

"May this gift, a reciprocal gift in nature, serve as an incessant reminder of the power of our brief statements, and the power of encouragement. You have serviced my journey because you caught me with pleasant surprise.

"You said something to me that I had not heard before. You have made a huge difference in the work phase of my life and in all other segments of my life."

Sufficiently Uncomfortable

I was to speak for one of the largest banks in our country. The audience was significant in number. The expectations were very high.

It is my custom to spend a considerable amount of time discussing with my clients what they hope to accomplish through my keynote presentation. My inquiry routinely includes two questions. When I had finish speaking, "How do you want the participants to feel? And, What do you want them to do?"

On this particular occasion, the meeting planner did not feel comfortable enough to answer those questions. She suggested a conference call between herself, the head of the department for which I was speaking, and me.

The lead person for this event was confident and articulate. I could sense it "over the telephone."

I was particularly intrigued and impressed by her answer to the first question: "How do you want your participants to feel upon leaving the presentation?"

She responded with several thoughts. The most significant thought, one that I have never heard before was, "I want our participants to leave feeling 'sufficiently uncomfortable.'"

I did have some questions about what that term meant. She would explain that term to me: "I want our participants to depart this conference feeling as if they have much difficult work to do, but also feeling as if they are inspired and prepared to do that difficult work."

What a Lesson

As I have written this book, I have felt, on many occasions, "sufficiently uncomfortable." I have felt both challenge and competent, both inadequate and filled with initiative, both irritated and inspired.

I suspect that many of you know what it means to feel "sufficiently uncomfortable." I am also aware that the content of this book probably, at certain mile markers, led you to feel sufficient, but uncomfortable.

Living with Struggle and Surprise

My hope is that *Traveling By Detour!* will minimize despair and enhance hope for you. I remind you, that although you are accountable for your choices, you have positioned beside you an arsenal of resources and an army of allies.

An Arsenal of Resources

"When I get a little money I buy books, and if any is left I buy food and clothes."
Erasmus

~

It is only two years ago that I recognized an interesting concept. The first four letters in "ready" are r-e-a-d. Books are certainly not the only component of your arsenal of resources. They are a key component.

The List of Books on the Subject that follow at book's end will prove helpful. Although I certainly do not concur with everything in each book, I have found them helpful within my life and in preparing for *Traveling By Detour!* It will be best if you seek affirmation from a psychiatrist/therapist/counselor as to the specific books that would benefit you the most. Do not take this suggestion lightly.

Remember, ready begins with r-e-a-d!

Your arsenal of resources is not limited to books. It is broad enough to include the internet, group therapy meetings, trade journals, and retreats.

An Army of Allies

As you seek to cope with struggle, it will be helpful if, in your Precious File of thoughts and references, you include supportive family members and friends. Do not merely include them, utilize them.

The truth is: I would not be writing this book if it were not for the continued support of my wife, my children, my sister, and my friends. This book is dedicated to Mr. Ron Seib for a reason. For more than a decade, he has been there for me as was indicated in the dedication page.

But Ron has not stood alone. Standing with him, and for me, has been my psychiatrist/therapist, Dr. Susanna Davis, my former pastor, Dr. Claude Smithmire, and a host of other friends including Dr. Wayne Livingston, Mr. Wade Hall, and Al Yancey.

My army of allies has been expanded by hundreds of clients across the country. Just yesterday, I relieved a "catch up call" from a client in Utah. My clients encourage me, pray for me, and bless me with perpetual surprise.

Please remember, you need not travel alone. There is, out there, an arsenal of resources. There also awaits for you, an army of allies.

I cannot conclude this segment without referring to The Buoy that has helped guide me through the detours. He has been both my hope and my help.

Living with Struggle and Surprise

Grace Who?

The setting was Emory University. I was a twenty-eight year old graduate student.

While pursuing advanced studies at Emory University Theological School, I was required to earn a certain number of credit hours in clinical training. This was not in the field of psychiatry, or any other area of medicine.

My clinical training was held at Egleston Children's Hospital. Daily, I would seek to minister to very sick children, and to their parents. Quite frankly, on most occasions, I did not know what to say or what to do.

On one particular afternoon, during a meeting with fellow students and with our supervisor, I was stunned. I could not believe what the supervisor said to me. I became very angry; that anger was both visible and expressed.

I had been attempting to express to the group and to the supervisor that I could not be enduring these days of "not knowing what to do" were not for the grace of God. At that point, the supervisor attacked! "Grace who?"

Not only did I feel attacked. I was also both confused and embarrassed. "What do you mean 'Grace who?'"

"What I mean is this: You have been speaking for weeks about grace in a non-chalant, impersonal, detached fashion. I don't think you know what Grace is. I fear that it is merely another word for you - that you are simply going through the theological motion of speaking the word."

Later in the afternoon, I rushed to the supervisor's office: "I am furious with you. Why would you say that? What right do you have to judge my feelings?"

He responded, "I have every right to monitor your feelings. I am your supervisor. And, I fear you have no idea in the world about what Grace really means."

I fear, upon decades of reflection, that he was correct. I knew how to form the word. I had not experienced the force behind the word. It was obvious to others.

I Now Know Better

After battling Obsessive-Compulsive Disorder and Bipolar Disorder for most of my life (knowingly since age forty-two), I have learned more about authentic grace. Initially, at approximately age forty-five, I began to experience brief glimpses of genuine grace.

It is only within the last few years that I have been able to experience authentic grace for expanded periods of time. My struggle at this point has been significant.

For most of my adult life, I have feared that the only way I would go to Heaven was if I did certain things in general, and if I became a missionary in particular. This fear has played a literal havoc within my life. The fear has been relentless.

Living with Struggle and Surprise

Off of the Cross

My first therapist was quick to identify this struggle as a major piece in my traveling by detour. I will never forget her words: "Stephen, the first thing we have to do is get you down off the cross."

I understand, and will teach to others, that we are saved by the grace of God, that Jesus hung on the cross to save us. But for decades, I have been hooked on this thought: "That this event does not apply to me."

I understand this is a flawed theology. I recognize that God's grace has sustained me in the midst of my misunderstanding. It is as if there are demons out there who constantly want to diffuse my energy, dwarf my creativity, and hold me in a state of hell on earth.

But year after year, albeit with significant interruptions, I have grown to appreciate much more of a "peace that passeth understanding." When I least expect it, when the detour path is long, and the struggle is deep, I am often caught off guard.

What catches me off guard is that which I do not deserve and cannot earn. It is Grace. I now know what it feels like - not all of the time, but some of the time.

I do not intend to be "preachy" at this point. My words emerge out from experience, not from theory. I know from whence my help cometh. I know who is my Supreme Ally.

Traveling By Detour!

A Whole New Level

You will never believe what happened today. I do not know whether it is attributed to my excitement about finishing this book, or it is associated with a lateral lock "on the up."

About an hour ago, I needed a break from the manuscript, and felt Heather, our executive assistant, needed a break from me. I shared with both Heather and my wife that "I had enjoyed about all of this I can stand, and needed a break."

I rushed to the car, and drove to the post office. It was not until I arrived at the post office that I recognized that I was wearing no shoes.

I hurriedly entered the post office and quickly departed. On the way toward my car, I noticed a gentleman working on the post office grounds. He wore the traditional post office blue and was clad in shorts. He was exhibiting a huge smile and a robust laughter.

This gentleman and I are good friends. We also hold something in common. We both wear shorts while at work. We have commented on numerous occasions about how comfortable we feel in our shorts.

I asked: "What is so funny?" He responded, "You have taken this comfort idea to a whole new level."

What follows on our last page is a significant reminder. The thought is this: "You and I can take our traveling by detour to a higher level."

Living with Struggle and Surprise

The Ultimate Surprise

In the game of tennis, there is a very interesting term. When the two players reach a unique state in the game, that situation is referred to as "deuce." "Deuce" is a tie-breaking event in which a player must score two successive points to win after the score is tied.

If a player scores the first of the required "two successive" points, that player receives the advantage. If Player A is battling Player B, and Player A is the first to score after "deuce," the official terminology is: Advantage: Player A.

Traveling by detour is something you and I have in common. Our detours vary at point of intensity and duration.

Our ultimate surprise is this: The advantage does not always have to lie at the feet of struggle. As you learn to anticipate, accept, analyze, apply, and appreciate what you have learned from traveling by detour, you can stack the advantage-odds in your favor. As you value recognition, resolve, response, reneging, regression, and re-visitation, you can bless yourself with surprise.

The story of *Traveling By Detour!* is this: You and I do not have to stay the way we are. We can live thusly: Advantage you; advantage me.

Struggle well!

~

Books On Subject List

Bodenburg, Dorothy A., M.F.C.C. *Overachieving Parents - Underachieving Children.* Los Angeles, CA: Lowell House, 1992

Carson, Ben. *Big Picture, The* Grand Rapids, Michigan: Zondervan Publishing House, 1999

Carter, Rosalynn with Golant, Susan. *Helping Someone With Mental Illness.* New York: Three Rivers Press, 1999

Castle, Lana R. *Bipolar Disorder Demystified.* New York: Marlowe & Company, 2003

Copeland, Mary Ellen.M.S, M.A. *Depression Workbook, The.* Oakland, CA: New Harbinger Publications, Inc., 2001

D'Antonio, Toni Raiten. *Velveteen Principles, The.* Deerfield Beach, FL: Health Communications, Inc. 2004

Fast, Julie A. with Preston, John D. PSYD, *Loving Someone With Bipolar Disorder.* Oakland, CA: New Harbinger Publications, 2004

Hansel, Tim. *When I Relax I Feel Guilty.* Elgin, IL: David C. Cook Publishing Co., 1979

Hansel, Tim. *You Gotta Keep Dancin'.* Elgin, IL: David C. Cook Publishing Co., 1985

Lewis, C.S. *Surprised By Joy.* Orlando, FL: Harcourt Brace Jovanich, 1956

Maxwell, John C. *Failing Forward*. Nashville: Thomas Nelson, Inc. 2000

McCulough, David. *Mornings On Horseback*. New York: Simon & Schuster Paperbacks, 2003

Moore, Thomas. *Care of the Soul*. New York: Harper Perennial, 1992

Munford, Paul R. *Overcoming Compulsive Checking*. New York: New Harbinger Publications, 2004

Nouwen, Henri J.M. with Durback, Robert, ed. *Seeds of Hope*. New York: Bantam Books, 1989

Nouwen, Henri J.M. *Wounded Healer, The*. Garden City, New York: Doubleday & Company, Inc. 1972

O'Connor, Richard, Ph.D. *Undoing Depression*. New York: Berkley Publishing Group, 1997

Remen, Rachel Naomi, M.D. *Kitchen Table Wisdom*. New York: Riverhead Books, 1996

Sherman, Doug with Hendricks, William. *Your Work Matters To God*. Colorado Springs, CO: Naupress, 1988

Skomal, Lenore. *Gratitude*. Maine: Cider Mill Press Book, 2006

About Stephen

Worldwide, Stephen M. Gower, CSP, is respected as "The Perception Professional." He works with organizations who want to lead change. He brings to the forefront an exploration and celebration of the remarkable relationship between individual team member choices and stellar team performance patterns. His unique blend of enthusiasm, experience, and content produces stunning results at the point of the passion behind change. His *What Do They See When They See You Coming?* book is recognized as the signature work on perception across the globe.

Earning a bachelor's degree from Mercer University and his master's degree from Emory University, Stephen has given more than 5,000 presentations and is a best selling author of seventeen books.

~

Contact Us:

For more information on Stephen's keynote speeches, workshops, consulting, and educational material:

smg@stephengower.com
800-242-7404

Printed in the United States
200072BV00005B/1-177/A

9 781880 150429